"*Step Into Your Vision* captures the essence of ⬛⬛⬛⬛ consultant I can testify that setting goals that ⬛⬛⬛⬛⬛ s critical to expediting success in your busines⬛⬛⬛⬛⬛ his level of commitment to her creativity and in ⬛⬛⬛⬛⬛ ⬛ job in capturing the concepts to succeed. App⬛, ⬛ ⬛ n take you to the next level!"
– Mark Katz, Chief Strategic Officer, www.Abusinessstrategy.com

"The information presented in *Step Into Your Vision* is conveyed in short, easy to read chapters. The content is relevant to anyone trying to implement or lead change."
– Steve M. Rosol, President/CEO of Mars Air Systems, www.marsair.com

"Setting goals is critical to becoming an Internet Millionaire. *Step into Your Vision* will teach you how to set and reach effective goals that can put more cash in your pocket."
– Tom Antion, Top Internet Marketer, www.GreatInternetMarketingTraining.com

"There are a lot of books on the market about self-improvement and achieving success. *Step Into Your Vision* condenses the best of principles from personal, real life experiences into one comprehensive, easy-to-read book that's sure to help you achieve your goals and live the life you deserve."
– Kelly Oliver, Real Estate Consultant, Tampa, Florida

"Don't settle for a mediocre life. Now is the time to Step Into YOUR Vision! This book will teach you how to take action, even in the face of fear."
– Alan Winters, Media Consultant, President of Winters Media Services,
  Los Angeles, California.

"Annette – Nice chapter. Well written. Your personal example makes it come alive. It's a process that works. Rock on!"
– Jack Canfield, CEO Jack Canfield Companies

"Jane Ann Covington shares the true secrets of success and happiness. She has taken a very complex topic and made it simple, yet profound. Her chapter Awaken Your Full Potential should be read, studied and practiced by all. I, for one, am grateful for her reminder. Thank you, Jane Ann, for sharing these brilliant yet simple insights with all of us."
– John Harricharan, award-winning author of the bestseller, *When You Can Walk on Water, Take the Boat*. www.KeysToInfinitePossibilities.com

"Debra Jones' brilliant chapter "True Wellness from the Inside Out" can empower you to find the strength from within to create the best version of yourself for a happier and healthier life."
– Kent Burden, Founder of My Life Fitness, www.mylifefitness.com

"Zenaida Roy-Almario definitely inspires change, while capturing the heart and soul of each and every reader – a phenomenal read! Her passion and commitment to inspire success in people definitely comes through in *Step Into Your Vision*."
– Mary E. Gilder, Author of "A Misrepresentation Of Myself" and Contributing Writer for Conversations Magazine, www.maryegilder.com

"There is something to be said about discovering your ability to overcome trials. Shamayah's chapter "The Art of Intention" truly brings home the point home in a way that speaks to many. As someone who also feeds off of the motivations in life, I found her chapter to be inspirational and educational. Her words are truly jewels to be treasured."
– Jonathan Milton, Tampa Bay Times fitness correspondent, St. Petersburg, Florida

"Stephen translates success formulas from concepts into actions in the real world. Stephen is not only a business catalyst, he inspires people to greatness. His impact transcends that bottom-line. Let his chapter "Good isn't Good Enough" make a change in your life!"
– Emmitt Summers, Vice President, Sales & Development Verengo Solar Plus, www.verengosolar.com

"Vision inspires one towards their potential, but taking action while applying course corrections along the way fuels the spirit of achievement. David Braun provides the roadmap to victory by revealing his Power Achievement Secrets in the must-have success manual *Step Into Your Vision*."
– Larry Broughton, Ernst & Young's Entrepreneur of the Year®, NaVOBA's Vetrepreneur® of the Year, best-selling author & keynote speaker, www.LarryBroughton.net

"Larry's chapter "Cruising Your Way to Success" weaves a story of adventure and pleasant fulfillment with flexible goals and planning. He shows that when we are open, we can find delight in the priceless surprises that living fully can bring."
– Richard Ritzenthaler, Designer, builder, inventor, music lover & longtime friend, Scottsdale, Arizona

"Having worked previously with Pauline in the insurance industry, I can attest to her professionalism and her passion for helping people meet their financial goals. In her chapter she carefully illustrates how to assess your needs, lay down a comprehensive foundation, and build a solid road map to get you from dreaming to actualization."
– Carol Roberts, Marketing Consultant & President, Board of Directors - Teresa Group

"I can attest to the fact that what Margaret teaches in "Co-Create with the Universe" works. Her processes are easy, practical and effective. Anyone would benefit from seeking her out and using her techniques for immediate results."
– Ruth Snow, Clutter Coach, Mill Valley, California

STEP into
your VISION

STEP into your VISION

Top Business Leaders Share Their Goal-Setting Secrets

Komera Press

ISBN #978-1-938474-00-2

Published by

Komera Press

138 107th Avenue, Suite 143, Treasure Island, Florida 33706

KomeraPress.com

Orders@KomeraPress.com

Cover photographs courtesy of www.dreamstime.com

TABLE OF CONTENTS

ACKNOWLEDGMENTS

With Gratitude....

A fantastic book like *Step Into Your Vision* can only be created with an amazing team!

First of all, there is gratitude to our creator, Jehovah God, who has given each one of us life and has provided us with the talents and gifts to be an inspiration for others.

A big thanks to Eric Lofholm and all the coauthors, especially John Assaraf and Greg S. Reid, for being so awesome and for being willing to share their awesomeness with the world by contributing to this book.

Then, there are the people behind the scenes, who have impacted my life tremendously:

To Tanya Sarrucco —

"Thank you for always supporting me to achieve my goals! You are the best sister in the world!"

To my Mom —

"Thank you for believing in me and for teaching me that everything is possible if you don't give up. You are a true inspiration."

To Catherine Spearmon —

"Catherine, you are the best! Thank you for creating this fantastic book with me and for your loyal support in challenging times."

I'm grateful for the love and support of my other sisters, Elmy, Terya and Sharryl. Thank you!

As I mentioned before, behind an amazing book like this stands an amazing team!

Thank you so much for your creativity, your commitment to excellence, your love, your care, your support and your willingness to share your expertise with me: Deborah Perdue, Lorna Romano, Jonathan Milton, Laura Latham, Gail Ransom, Mark Katz, Aneissa van Metre, Marsha Evans, Loral Langemeier, Saundra White, Jeanne Johnson, Ryn Dietz, Jeanne & Mike Asaro, Daniel Ross, Nadege Bryant, Edna & Ed Terry, Martise Armstrong and Donald Hunter.

Shamayah

Foreword

*O*ver the years, I have created thousands of millionaires. Yet, how many people don't have a goal of becoming a millionaire? Thousands of people are given the same resources and tools, but they give up before they achieve their goals. What is the difference? Why do some people make up their minds what they want and succeed, where others don't seem to get ahead in life?

You are reading this book because you are looking to create the life you WANT to live instead of being stuck in a routine. It is time to say "Yes!" to what you do want and stop whining and complaining about how bad the economy is. It is this YES! Energy that gives you extreme optimism, creates new opportunities and builds momentum to start living the life you really want.

Whether it comes from our family, friends, or professional lives, we are often "trained" out of the ability to dream and achieve our goals. Somewhere in the past, many of us were taught limiting beliefs that have been holding us back. You may have heard, "No, you can't do that!" so often you have started to believe it. Well, it's time to leave your past behind you, get rid of toxic friends and surround yourself with people who will say, "Yes! I believe in you."

Step Into Your Vision gives you the guidance and direction you need to overcome your limiting beliefs and create a specific, step-by-step plan that is in alignment with your true self. When you are in alignment, all areas of your life are part of a unified purpose or mission. Don't engage in an activity that contradicts another, because this conflict will drain your energy. Instead, continue to gain, build, and grow.

Eric Lofholm and Shamayah Sarrucco have done an amazing job in bringing you a truly empowering compilation of valuable goal-setting lessons. Let the stories of the coauthors inspire you to say, "Yes! I commit to my goals." But it's not just about having goals. It's not just about writing them down or visualizing them. It is about you committing to do whatever it takes. It's not rocket science—if you want to achieve your goals, you need to be committed, stay focused and take action every day. You won't get anywhere if you don't take action. Don't be afraid to fail or make mistakes. Just say, "Yes!" and figure it out. Of course, it is helpful to learn from other people's mistakes so you can reduce the pitfalls. You can't be successful as a "lone ranger." That is why I recommend you take advantage of the wealth of knowledge the experts in this book share. Take the fast track to achieving your goals!

What would your life look like if you knew you truly had a choice? Where would you like to be in six months, a year or even five years from now? So many people get sloppy with their goals. They expect their lives and their finances to get better, yet they don't make the changes required. How you spend your time and your energy day after day, week after week, month after month, will determine your future.

Shift your intention to the energy you want to have. Apply the strategies and principles in this incredible book and live the life you deserve!

Just say YES!

Loral Langemeier

Introduction

"*I am going to be a fireman,*" "*I want to be a pilot,*" "*When I grow up, I'll buy a Ferrari.*" Didn't we all have big dreams and great ideas for our lives when we were young? There were no limits to what we believed was possible—the world was one huge playground in which to play and have fun!

Unfortunately, many people allowed their dreams to fade over time. Some of us might have even forgotten about these beautiful desires in our hearts. On occasion, we may look back and wonder what happened. Where did the time go and why did our dreams go by unfulfilled? Why do so many find it difficult to make their vision of the future into reality? How can you turn your dreams into goals and take practical steps toward a successful, happy and fulfilling life? Well, this book is not about mere dreaming. The 32 experts in this book will reveal their secrets to help you create the life you deserve. Even when you don't know exactly what you would like your life to look like, this book can have a great impact on your life.

We all think we are unique in what we are going through in life and the challenges we've had to face. Yes, we are unique, yet many more people than you think face the same challenges you do. That is why everybody is touched by the achievements of someone who makes his dreams come true. When Barack Obama became the first black president of the U.S., it gave hope to millions of people. His famous, "Yes, we can!" resonated inside of us. In our hearts, a soft voice said, "Well, if he can do it, maybe I can, too." The soft voice used to be loud and clear. As a kid, we had no difficulty listening to our hearts telling us our deepest desires and wishes. We were not afraid to share our dreams with the world. Yet, little by little we chose the voice of others above the voice of our own hearts. We told ourselves, "It's safer. They'll like us. It's easier." We allowed others to tell us what we could or couldn't do, instead of trusting our own intuition, talents and skills. For some of us the voice has stopped talking, making us believe we don't have a dream or that our dream is impossible to achieve, even though deep inside there is still this longing to share our gifts with the world.

Most of us have never been taught how the goal-setting process works. Others have become hesitant or even afraid to dream or set goals for fear of disappointment. Yet, the pain of not reaching for your goal is greater than the *potential* pain of not succeeding the first time, because that is what it is: *potential* pain, only. When you follow the goal-setting principles in this book, you will discover that you can succeed at anything you set your mind to, but it may not happen right away. You may fall and have to get up a couple of times. (Or you may conclude that your initial goal was not what you truly wanted and end up with something even better.) Yes, it may be painful when you don't succeed the first time, but playing small and not living up to your true potential is much worse. Just like a plant is either growing or dying, you are either moving towards or away from your goals—there is no status quo.

Some people may have been numbed by life to the point that they aren't even aware they've given up. If that is you, then don't despair; *Step Into Your Vision* can reignite the fire inside of you. Even if it's nothing more than a smoldering wick at this point, the stories from these authors can rekindle in you that flame-like desire to create a better life for yourself—and it's not too late. No matter your age or your circumstances, you can start on your journey to an extraordinary life today. Because as soon as you start your journey, your life will change. As the expression goes, "Happiness isn't a destination, it's a journey." It is living each and every day with joy, knowing that you are on the right path. It's living your true self, complete with all its challenges and victories, inspiring others around you to open up to the greatness inside of them.

Take, for instance, Ramesh Kumar, MD. In his chapter, he shares how he was kicked out of his own practice and left empty-handed, with a huge debt. He could have let that experience kill his dream of helping patients, embitter him and cause him to give up. Instead, he got back on his feet. He learned the skills he needed to succeed as a business owner, which he wasn't taught in medical school, has built a state-of-the-art practice and now motivates and teaches other physicians entrepreneurial skills. He bounced back, despite the magnitude of the challenge he was facing, because he refused to let anything come between him and his goals.

Then there's Ryn Deitz, who empowers people to have fun while improving their financial lives. If your goal involves having more money to enjoy life and provide for your family, her chapter will show you how to take a different approach towards manifesting money, making it fun and exciting!

As Wayne Kotomori shares in his chapter, hope is vital in achieving your goals—even 0.00000001% is better than none. Hope is what keeps you from giving up. It's what kept Samira Bachir from giving up when the doctors told her she had six months to live. Her experience can teach us to treasure every moment of our lives, to not take anything for granted.

John Assaraf has spoken about the importance of visualization many times. In this book, he will help you to see why it works and what it teaches us about ourselves, as well as how you can use it to achieve your goals and bring yourself into closer alignment with your true self. After you visualize, though, then what? You can't just sit around and think about what you want and expect everything to just fall out of the sky into your lap. Eric Lofholm's 10-step goal-setting process will teach you exactly how to use the power of visualization and take the right actions to achieve your goals.

This is just a small sampling of what lies in store for you in the pages of this book. Each one of the authors is excited to share with you the secrets that have worked for them. Some of them have dealt with tremendous challenges and setbacks, yet somehow they found a way to turn the challenges into opportunities. Take, for example, JoAnn Oppenheimer, who uses her own experiences of going through divorce, losing the love of her life and her only son in a terrible car accident to support and encourage others, coaching them how to find the sunshine behind the clouds. She is a true inspiration and a great example that no matter how tough life gets, you can always choose how you deal with your circumstances.

What's more, know that you are not on your own. They say, "When the student is ready, the teacher appears." Well, I would like to introduce you to the most amazing teachers you will find. Each one of them would love to help you on your journey. So if you resonate with their messages, feel free to contact them and share your story with them. (And, when you have an inspirational, empowering story yourself, email books@coauthorswanted.com. We would love to hear from you!)

It is the foremost hope of all of us that you will create an incredible life and Step Into *Your* Vision.

CHAPTER I

The 10-Step Goal Setting Process – To Create the Life of Your Dreams

Eric Lofholm

> *"Though no one can go back and make a brand new start, anyone can start from now and make a brand new ending."*

*G*oal setting is one of the most misunderstood personal development ideas. At a personal development seminar I attended, the speaker shared his insight on goal setting. He asked the attendees, "How many of you consider yourselves goal setters?" 99% of the people in the audience raised their hands. He then said, "Let's find out. Take out a clean sheet of paper. Write down 10 goals. You have three minutes. GO."

Just like everybody else, I began to write. At the end of the three minutes, I only had seven goals. I was surprised: I was not able to come up with 10. The speaker then asked the group, "How many of you were able to come up with 10 goals?" About 50 hands went up, even though there were over 1,000 people in the room. Only 5% were able to complete this simple exercise. He explained that the reason most of us were unable to complete the exercise was because we were not goal setters. "For a goal to be a goal, it must be written down. Most people think that goal setting is merely deciding what you want. That is only the first step. Goal setting is a process. If you are not following the process, then what you are doing is not goal setting." He taught us his process and I was fascinated, because all along I thought I had been goal setting, and I realized in that moment that I had not.

After that day, I continued to study goal setting. I collected the most powerful and successful principles in the world and used them to create my own 10-step goal-setting process that will teach you quickly and easily how to create the life of your dreams.

Why should I set goals and write them down?

Many people believe they are goal setters, yet they fail to write down their goals.

Here are nine reasons why you should write down your goals:

1 **Written goals help you reduce stress by creating a compelling future for you.** Stress is often caused by fear of what might happen. As the future only exists in your imagination, why not imagine a bright, compelling future?

2 **Written goals guide you to move in the right direction.** Suppose you are at the pier in San Francisco and are getting ready to take a trip. There are three boats: A luxury liner to Alaska, a fishing boat to Japan and a private yacht to Los Angeles. Your goal is to get to Japan—which boat do you board? Of course, the fishing boat headed to Japan, even though it is the least luxurious of the three and would take the longest time. In spite of that, you would still take the fishing boat because it would help you reach your destination.

3 Written goals activate your subconscious mind. Have you ever gone to bed thinking about a problem, and then in the middle of the night, you awoke with the answer? That is your subconscious mind working for you. It has a tremendous influence on your behavior. An iceberg is a great metaphor for the power of your subconscious mind. Above the surface, you can only see the tip of the iceberg—your conscious mind. If you would go under the water, though, you would see a much larger mass of ice—your subconscious mind.

4 Written goals help you clearly communicate your life plans to others. Many of the goals you have will require the assistance and cooperation of others. One skill you will need to develop is the ability to clearly communicate your goals to others. When you go through the process of writing down your goals, you improve your ability to communicate your goals to yourself and others.

5 Written goals increase the likelihood that you will achieve your goals by 1000%. A great example to which many people can relate is a wedding. When you planned your wedding, did you write down your goals? And do you believe that effort increased the probability that your wedding plans would be realized? Without the written goals, the overall plan for the wedding would have been lost.

6 Written goals clarify how to invest your time. Goals give your life direction and help you to know where to focus your time and energy. If your goal is to become the top real estate agent in your area, are you likely to have a job as a receptionist? No, of course not; you will have a job as a real estate agent. Many people have jobs that are not helping them achieve their dreams, because they have never taken the time to think about what they want and write it down.

7 **Written goals motivate you.** As a sales coach, I have met thousands of salespeople who hate to make cold calls. On a scale of 1 to 10, their motivation to make sales calls is 1. I have also met many salespeople who are extremely motivated to make cold calls. What is the difference between the two? I have found that the motivated salespeople focus on the benefits they are receiving by making the cold calls. In other words, they have invested the time to clearly communicate to themselves the specific benefits they are receiving by making the calls. When you have written goals, you have a plan in writing that communicates to you the benefits you are going to receive once you take action.

8 **Written goals help you attract what you want.** Have you ever had a goal that manifested? When we moved into our house, we wanted a new kitchen table. Within 30 days of writing down that goal, our friend, Mark, offered us a brand new kitchen table with four matching chairs, for free. Events like this happen every day. Test it out. Be very clear on what you want and follow the 10-step goal-setting process and see what happens. Sometimes results come without effort, but of course, I'm not suggesting that you don't take consistent action.

9 **Written goals help you create the life of your dreams.** Why did you purchase this book? Why are you investing the time to learn these proven principles? For most people, the answer is to help you create the life of your dreams. Every successful person is applying these proven principles in her or his life. The goal setting principles are proven—like gravity, they always work. You must first clearly define the life of your dreams. Then you must write it down, create a plan of action and take action.

By now, you clearly see the benefits of goal setting. You realize that this is the one strategy consistently used by the most successful people in the world, and you may wonder why everyone doesn't use goal setting as a strategy to realize their dreams.

The 9 reasons people don't set goals:

☆ **They don't know the importance of goal setting.**

The main benefit of goal setting is that it will help you get anything you want in life faster and easier than without goals. Once people realize how important goal setting is, they immediately become goal setters.

☆ **They don't know how.**

Most people have never been taught proper goal-setting techniques.

☆ **They think they are already doing it.**

Many people think goal setting is merely deciding what you want, but that is only the first step of the 10 steps.

☆ **They don't have any goals.**

In reality, everyone has dreams or goals. Yet not everyone has taken the time to really think about what they want most in life, write it down, create a plan for achievement and then take action.

☆ **They are afraid of failure.**

Many people have the vision and the goals, but they never take action because the thought of failure dominates their minds. My suggestion is to set small goals using proper goal-setting techniques. Once your confidence is up and you see how easy it is, you can move on to bigger goals.

☆ **They don't believe in themselves.**

Our beliefs shape our behavior. In most cases, we only attempt what we believe we can achieve. Goal setting is not a belief exercise. Goal setting is an exercise in clearly defining what you want, writing it down, creating a plan for achievement and taking action.

☆ **They suffer from the curse of early success.**

For some, success comes easy at an early age. And then life deals them a blow, as life does. They lose that unstoppable confidence they had, and they give up.

☆ **They are in a comfort zone.**

Many people are comfortable where they are in their lives. They have no desire to strive for more out of life. Do you truly have what you want out of life, or are you settling for less?

☆ **They are afraid of success.**

You may have a big goal, like becoming the CEO of a Fortune 500 company. Then suddenly you think about the responsibilities that will come with it and you become fearful. Do you have goals that you are not pursuing because you fear the consequences if you succeed?

The 10-step goal-setting process

When I designed this process, I wanted to combine the most effective goal-setting strategies with the easiest application. While I was creating this system, many of the processes I looked at were either too complicated or didn't give you enough information to be effective. The following system is designed with you in mind. Follow the 10 simple steps in order, and turn your dreams into reality.

1 **Think about what you want, and write it down.** What is your dream? Where do you want to travel in your lifetime? How much money do you want to have when you retire? What would be the ideal job? The goal-setting process starts with thinking about what you want and how you want your life to be. One simple way to get started is by asking questions.

Assume I want to lose weight. I have low energy and poor eating habits. During the brainstorming session, I ask myself several health-related questions like, for example, "How do I want to feel when I wake up in the morning? What would my ideal weight be? What type of foods do I want to put into my body? What foods should I be avoiding?" My answers are my thought menu: "I want to feel energized when I wake up in the morning. My ideal body weight is 185 pounds. I want to eat more fruits and vegetables. I should avoid fast food, ice cream and soda."

2 **Decide exactly what you want, and write it down.** The second step in goal setting is to decide exactly what you want. Be as specific as you can. For example, write down "I want to earn $100,000 over the next 12 months" instead of "I want to make more money next year." That would not be specific enough.

This is what the thought menu from our example looks like:
  – I want to feel energized when I wake up in the morning.
  – My ideal body weight is 185 pounds.
  – I want to eat more fruits and vegetables.
  – I will avoid fast food, ice cream and soda.

From this thought menu, I want to take one idea to its completion. I decide the specific goal I want to achieve is to weigh 185 pounds. I now weigh 238, so my goal is to lose 53 pounds.

3 **Make sure your goal is measurable.** For a goal to be a goal, it must be written down. Once you have written it down, look at your goal to see if it is measurable—you will know when you have accomplished your goal. In our example, my goal is to weigh 185 pounds. That is measurable, so it passes the test. If your goal is not measurable, go back to Step 2 and rewrite your goal, making sure that it is measurable.

4 **Identify the specific reasons you want this goal, and write them down.** The reason most people fail to achieve their goals is that they don't have a compelling enough reason to achieve them. Once you have begun the 10-step goal-setting process, you are ready to take action. Along the path toward achieving your goals, you are going to run into some obstacles. That is where your **why** comes in. If your reason for achieving the goal is greater than the obstacles you face, then you will be much more likely to achieve the goal. Here is an example: You have been smoking a pack of cigarettes per day for 18 years. You have had a goal to quit smoking for the last six years because you know smoking isn't good for you. You followed proper goal-setting techniques. You tried hypnosis, gum and quit-smoking seminars. Nothing seemed to work. You go to the doctor. The doctor says you have lung cancer. If you quit smoking now, you will have 10 years to live. If you keep smoking, you will die in one year. Would you be able to quit smoking? I think you (and most people) would. Even though it was a goal of yours for the last six years and you were unable to succeed, I believe you would be able to quit. You would have a strong enough reason to accomplish the goal.

When you set a goal, look at **why** you want to achieve the goal. Is your **why** a big enough reason for you to overcome the obstacles to achieving your goal? If you don't have a strong enough reason, then imagine one. Spend some time really thinking about what it would mean to you to accomplish the goal. Also think about what the consequences would be if you didn't accomplish the goal.

Write a paragraph about why you will succeed in achieving your goal. Once you have completed the paragraph, read it over. Then ask yourself the question, "Do I have a big enough **why** to overcome the obstacles I am going to encounter?"

Back to my weight-loss example. Here is my **why**: "I must lose 53 pounds because this is not the person I really am. I am sick and tired of people thinking of me as fat. I want to run a marathon before I die, and I will never be able to do it at this weight." I then look at my paragraph. I believe I have a strong enough reason to overcome the obstacles I am going to face, so I continue with the process. If your **why** is not compelling enough, you must go back and rewrite it.

5 **Establish a definite date for accomplishment of your goal, and write it down.** It is very important to decide when you want to accomplish your goal. Your mind has an unconscious timeline in it. For example, if your goal is to graduate from college by the end of 2014, your mind needs to start working on plans for how you will make that happen. Knowing when you want to accomplish your goal will also have an effect on how you plan to achieve it. For example, if your goal is to earn $100,000 in the next 12 months, that is very different from having a goal of earning $100,000 any time in the future. Once you write down an end date for your goal, your mind will start working toward achieving it. The only way to take advantage of your mind is to set a date and enter it into your subconscious by writing it down. In our weight-loss example, my goal is to lose 53 pounds by March 25, 2012 (6 months from today).

6 **List the action steps you need to take to accomplish your goal, and write them down.** Ask yourself, "What are all of the steps I need to take to accomplish my goal?" This is a brainstorming exercise. Here we are looking to capture as many ideas as possible. We call this the action steps menu. Once again, we want as many choices as possible to create our plan. We are not looking for the steps to be in order at this point. Take out a clean sheet of paper and write anything and everything that comes to mind—things you will need to do in order to achieve your goal. This is my action steps menu for our weight loss example:

– Go to the health food store to get good food.

– Exercise three times per week.

– Take a multi-vitamin every day.

– Meet with a nutrition expert to establish a diet.

– Meet with an exercise specialist to create a workout program.

– Create a tracking system to track my results.

– Buy an exercise book.

– Talk to my friend, Bob (Bob lost 30 pounds last year), to find out how he lost weight.

Notice that the list is not in any particular order. This is a brainstorming session. I am looking to capture as many ideas as I can on paper. Once I have listed as many ideas as I can think of, I will then go to the next step.

7 **Create an action plan from your list of action steps, and write it down.** Step 7 is where your thoughts mesh into a plan. Look at your action steps from Step 6. Put those ideas in sequential order. First, do this. Then, do that. All we are doing to create our plan is to prioritize the action steps in Step 6. Do not let the word **plan** scare you. This is a simple exercise.

1. Talk to my friend, Bob (Bob lost 30 pounds last year), and find out how he lost weight.

2. Buy an exercise book.

3. Make an appointment to meet with a nutrition expert to establish a diet.

4. Make an appointment to meet with an exercise specialist to create a workout plan.

5. Meet with the nutrition expert.

6. Go to the health food store to get good food.

7. Take a multi-vitamin every day.

8. Meet with the exercise specialist.

9. Create a tracking system to track my results.

10. Exercise three times per week.

Most people think creating an action plan is a lengthy process. The word plan scares them. As you can see from the above example, the plan took only a few minutes of thought. When you create a plan to achieve a goal, you need to ask yourself, "If I follow the plan, will I achieve the goal?" So in our example, if I execute the plan, can I lose 53 pounds in six months? The answer is yes.

> *"The big secret in life is that there is no big secret.*
> *Whatever your goal, you can get there,*
> *if you're willing to work."*
> – Oprah Winfrey

8 **Take action.** Every step in the 10-step goal-setting process is important. Each step depends upon the others. This step, however, could be the most important. I can't tell you how many educated derelicts I have met over the years—you know, the people who know everything about everything, yet can't seem to get themselves to take action in their own lives. Goals and plans are great, but they don't produce results.

The only thing that produces results is action. How many times have you planned to do something, yet when it came to the action phase, you didn't act? You must get yourself to take consistent action on a daily basis, even if it is baby action steps. Remember: Inch by inch, it's a cinch. When you take action on a consistent basis, even if it is a small step, you take advantage of the law of momentum. The law of momentum states that a body in motion, once in motion, tends to stay in motion.

In our weight-loss example, one action I might take today is to go to the health food store and pick out some food. That is a positive step toward the achievement of my goal. It is a small step. This step will help me create momentum. Another step I might take is to jog for two minutes today. That might not seem like a lot, but it really is. Most people never achieve their goals because they never take the first step. They never benefit from the law of momentum. Remember, the journey of a thousand miles begins with just one step. Inch by inch, it's a cinch.

9 **Do something every day.** Work toward the achievement of your goals every day, even if you only take a small step. Rome wasn't built in a day, and your major life goals aren't going to happen overnight in most cases. Practice patience. In our weight-loss example, "Today I will make an appointment with Bob to find out how he was able to lose weight." This action may seem like a small step toward the achievement of my goal, yet it will activate the law of momentum. By taking this small step today, I have put the law of momentum in my favor.

10 **View your goals as often as possible.** Out of sight, out of mind— human beings don't have the best memories. You have invested time to complete Steps 1 through 9. Now that your goals are written down with a plan, you can quickly review 5 to 10 goals in a matter of minutes. The more frequently you view your goals, the more you will burn them into your subconscious mind. Something magical happens when you do that. After some time of frequently reviewing your goals with their plans of action, your subconscious mind will believe you are going to achieve them. Once you have accomplished that, you can take advantage of the most powerful personal development idea ever discovered: We become what we think about.

Notice, with the exception of Step 8 (take action), every step requires that you think about what you want. Remember: We become what we think about. This is one of the secrets of this 10-step process. It requires that you invest time thinking about what you want most in your life.

Many people who do not achieve their goals invest their time thinking of all the reasons they can never succeed in their lives, or they invest their time thinking of ways to solve other peoples' problems, or they invest their time thinking about the fact that they have no money. Note there is nothing wrong with thinking about these things. However, if you choose to invest your time thinking in this way, just realize the consequences. Remember: We become what we think about.

The Author's Challenge to You

You have just learned the most powerful goal-setting process in the world. I challenge you to take action, to implement these proven principles and create the life of your dreams.

— ABOUT THE AUTHOR —

Eric Lofholm is a Master Sales Trainer who has trained tens of thousands of sales professionals nationwide. His clients have added millions of dollars to their sales bottom line after attending Eric's energetic and groundbreaking seminars. Ever since the beginning of his career in sales, he has maintained a track record of outperforming his fellow sales reps. He has been trained by top trainers like Anthony Robbins and Dr. Donald Moine, Ph.D., and many of America's top companies hire Eric regularly to train, motivate, and inspire their sales teams. www.saleschampion.com.

"Balance is knowing
when to intend,
When to have a goal
and fight for it,
And when to surrender,
letting go of all expectations,
In full faith that the highest
and best will happen."

– Shamayah

CHAPTER 2

The Art of Intention

Shamayah Sarrucco

> *"In the morning sow your seed and until*
> *the evening do not let your hand rest;*
> *for you are not knowing where this will*
> *have success, either here or there, or whether*
> *both of them will alike be good."*
> – Ecclesiastes 11:6

"Can you hear me?" "Can you open your eyes?" Even though I can't see anything, I can feel more and more people crowding around me.

"Are you okay?" a concerned woman asks. What a question! Why would I be lying on the cold floor of the hotel lobby if I was okay?

When the paramedics arrive, they ask me, "Can you open your eyes?" I understand that this is part of the procedure. But seriously, are there people who keep their eyes closed until the paramedics get there?

"Can you hear me?" "What is her name?" Someone answers, "Shamayah," and the paramedic asks, while he checks my heart beat, "Shamayah, are you in pain?" I can hear everything they say, and I am aware of everything that happens around me, but no matter how hard I try, I can't move, I can't talk, I can't open my eyes.

I'm a healthy young woman, and here I am on the lobby floor of the Westin Hotel, totally paralyzed. Weird. It's a little scary. There's nothing I can do. As soon as I decide to stop struggling and to surrender to the moment, I feel more peaceful.

Have you ever felt knocked down on the ground? When you felt that no matter how much effort you put into it, you were not moving—you were totally stuck? Maybe you felt so overwhelmed with the situation that you didn't know what to do or say, or perhaps you had demanded too much of your body, and were so exhausted, you had a hard time concentrating and getting things done.

The paramedics picked me up and put me in the ambulance that took me to the hospital. It was a strange experience. I remember thinking, "I am too young for these crazy things to happen to me." I had to stay overnight so they could do more tests the next day. Several hours later, I was able to slowly move again and by the next day, I was doing better. It took a couple of months before I was able to function normally again. Despite the EEG, MRI, blood tests, X-rays and other tests, the doctors could not tell me what had caused me to collapse, but the experience guided me to a new path.

Whenever life hits you hard, you need to make a choice: you can retreat, blame life and get bitter, or you can search for the gift in the pain and discover valuable lessons. You can't choose your circumstances, but you can choose how you respond to them. Most successful people have a special skill that sets them apart; they know "The Art of Intention." They go with the flow, they remain open to possibilities, yet are prepared to face challenges. They understand that obstacles aren't something that should stop you. Instead, they're opportunities to become more creative! Learning the art of intention can enrich your life beyond your imagination, and add a lot of fun, joy and happiness to everything you do. Let's pick up the brush and get started...

"One of the secrets of life is to make
stepping stones out of stumbling blocks."
– Jack Penn

Art Lesson #1. Love Yourself

As humans, we can have a tendency to believe that we are invincible. Especially as business owners, we often demand a great deal of ourselves because we have big dreams and big goals. We are willing to do "whatever it takes." Sometimes we can get so caught up in achieving our goals that we might forget to be present in the moment and enjoy the journey. I had been so focused on achieving my goals that I had lost sight of me.

The essence is that you have to **LOVE** yourself unconditionally to **BE** the person, who will **DO** what is needed, in order to **HAVE** your dreams manifested. When you get the order mixed up, everything becomes much more complicated. My mentors taught me the importance of learning to love myself. The more you love yourself, the better you'll take care of yourself, the better your energy, the stronger your intention and the easier you'll attract the people, opportunities and situations to help you achieve your goals.

You can't make the grass grow faster by pulling it. It takes time to overcome childhood wounds. Maybe you need to find somebody who can guide you on your path. Our parents did the best they could with the resources they had, but their own limiting beliefs and dysfunctional upbringing may have affected you more than you realize, no matter how loving and caring they were. You have to trust and be patient. Allow yourself time to learn and to grow, becoming a better person every day. Believe in yourself and you can make the impossible happen!

"Life is a precious gift.
Don't get caught up in the wrapping paper."
– Shamayah Sarrucco

Art Lesson #2. Live Your Values

What is truly important in your life? What do you want to be known for? How do you want to be remembered? What are your values? You probably have been asked these questions before. Did you take the time to define the answers? Your values define the core of your being, and living them will create the right balance in your life. Make a commitment to yourself to define your values within the next week. (It's ok to refine them over time, but you have to start somewhere.) When you are in alignment with your values, you'll be energized from the inside out.

Set your intention based on your values, and use your values as the foundation to determine your goals. Sometimes you may not be totally clear on your goals. Other times you may discover that there is a better path to take than the one you thought was right. Or you may realize that you have received something much more valuable than the goal you had set. As long as you know your intention and stay in alignment with your values, your life will unfold in miraculous ways, bringing you joy and happiness.

Being clear on my values shifted the focus of my life. I came to realize that I wasn't living my true self, because my life and business didn't reflect my values. My priorities had been messed up and it had affected my health to the extent that I ended up in the hospital. Since I have started to truly live my values, I am celebrating every step of my journey and I am experiencing a joy and inner peace beyond compare.

My personal values are also the values of my company. I use them as guidelines to select my clients, my joint venture partners and my team:

♥ Spirituality

Serving Jehovah God first and living Bible principles. These include keeping integrity, being honest and showing compassion, to name just a few of these principles.

♥ Love

Genuinely caring and wanting the best for the people around us—
Our family, friends, our team, our clients and their clients, all those whose
lives we want to touch.

♥ Passion

Being excited about life and the work we do—having a smile in our
heart that reflects on our face. Living our true self and developing our full
potential, inspiring others to do the same.

♥ Commitment to Excellence

Striving to be outstanding in whatever we do by setting a higher
standard. Knowing that good is not good enough, we continue to
"sharpen" each other and go the extra mile.

"Always remember, you are here to love, laugh,
heal the world and fly beyond your wildest dreams..."
– Shamayah Sarrucco

Art Lesson #3. Strengthen Your Intention

Some say that you are born an artist—or not. One art teacher wanted to
prove that statement wrong. She took a random group of people and had
them create a painting. It looked like the work of six-year-olds! She taught
them the basic principles and over time, several of them became such great
artists that they were selling their work. The same is true if you want to
master the art of intention: even though some may be more talented than
others, it is a skill you can learn.

Character and perseverance will determine what you will do after you
have set your intention. Focusing on your intention, taking action, and
achieving your goals is not a one-time event—it is a daily habit, a way of

living. What can help you accomplish this? Everything shapes your view of the world, your mindset and your beliefs. Look at young children. They pick up a new language from their peers by osmosis.

☆ Be selective in the people you spend time with

The people around you have a tremendous impact on who you become. Their comments, actions and beliefs can build you up or tear you down. Be careful to surround yourself with friends who believe in you, who give you a hand to pull you up again when you are facing setbacks, who cheer you on and encourage you to keep going—who won't allow you to give up. Their expectations will affect the expectations you have of yourself.

☆ Fill your mind with empowering thoughts

When you master your thoughts, you master your life. Your thoughts build your beliefs. The more confident you are, the more likely you are to stick to your goals and be persistent. Read books, listen to music and watch movies that show the greatness that is in each one of us. This will inspire you to go beyond your current reality and overcome any fears that may come up.

☆ Make every day count

You need to develop the habit of doing things every day that will bring you closer to your goal, whether you feel like it or not. In his book *Today Matters*, John C. Maxwell brings out, "You will never change your life until you change something you do daily." You can't just set a goal: you need to learn the skills to achieve it and work every day to become better at it.

You may have heard stories of people who say they set an intention and a miracle happened, out of the blue—this is rarely the case. Before they could enjoy the fruits, they had to grow the roots of their tree. Success is a process. It is in the small steps you take every day. Everything has an effect on you.

It may seem small, but over time the compounded effect of all the little choices you have made will determine the outcome of your life. It requires discipline. Yet knowing that you are living your true self by developing your full potential will give you satisfaction and joy.

> *"Make each day your masterpiece."*
> – John Wooden

Art Lesson #4. Become a Diamond

Life doesn't happen in a linear manner. This is important to understand, because it will help you to be prepared for obstacles that you'll have to overcome in order to achieve your goal. Success doesn't come overnight. To the outside world it may look that way, but those who have traveled the path know better. You don't wake up one morning and decide to run a marathon without any training. It takes dedication, preparation and perseverance to make it to the finish. Achieving your goals is like finally winning the gold medal: you sacrificed blood, sweat and tears; you were up early in the morning, even if you didn't feel like it; you fought your own thoughts and doubts when reality seemed to prove that you were never going to make it. When you win, nobody sees beyond that moment of glory—the many years of hard work, the many nights you prayed in desperation, the many battles you lost to win this war. Whenever you feel like giving up, remember the words from Napoleon Hill: *"Most great people have attained their greatest success just one step BEYOND their greatest setback and failure."*

Regardless of what happened—whether you were fighting to keep your marriage, your business, your job, your home, or your health—it is understandable to feel defeat if things didn't work out the way you expected. In every battle, people get wounded. Some of them get bitter and resentful, because they feel life is unfair. . . and you know, sometimes it is. But that is no excuse to give up. Others move on with their lives after they have experienced disappointment, more cautious than before, more guarded, more skeptical. When they have positive experiences, they may soften and slowly start to heal. Very few people transform themselves and use their painful experience as an opportunity to learn and grow as a person. They become like the chunk of coal that takes advantage of the tremendous pressure and the heat of the circumstances to become a diamond. Just like diamonds are formed under extreme geological conditions—when the temperature is 800 degrees Celsius and the pressure is 50,000 times atmospheric pressure, deep below the surface of the earth (150-200 km)—it is often in the lowest times of your life that you can learn the most valuable lessons. The challenges you have faced and the flexibility you needed to overcome them can help you grow as a person, and your life experience can help you become "more precious."

> *"Success isn't something you achieve,*
> *it's what you attract by the person you become."*
> – Jim Rohn

Art Lesson #5. Write, Inspire, Prosper

It has been several months since I had my "wake up call." I've had my life shaken up a couple more times since then and have discovered that in the devastating pain of the emotions, you can't see beyond that moment, as if you are thrown into a bottomless black hole. Regardless of how bad the situation may be, you always have a choice: You can choose to feel sorry for yourself and stay in your victim role, or you can master your thoughts and step out. You have the choice to fight or to surrender. It took me a little while to discover that fighting reality is as ridiculous as fighting the weather, and that I was only exhausting myself in the process. As soon as I stopped fighting and surrendered, amazing things happened. Patience and acceptance are key qualities to develop.

We have to accept life as it comes by setting goals, without being attached to the outcome, because when you hold on too tight and don't allow life to flow, you miss out on what is really important. Unfortunately, we're not taught to create our lives with this kind of gentleness. It's easy to just have one idea and know exactly how it needs to be accomplished and all of the steps along the way, but if you have a rigid view of how you are going to accomplish your goal, it will be much harder to reach it.

Sometimes you want to climb the mountain. You are ready: You have read the books, listened to the motivational cd's, and are confident you can make it happen. Only God doesn't want you to climb the mountain, He wants you to go around the mountain. So don't set a goal that is unyielding in its execution; rather, remain flexible.

Mastering the art of intention—allowing, being open to possibility and listening to God's guidance—will let you achieve something much greater than you ever could have thought: Miracles will happen! Seemingly strange coincidences will occur in which you'll be in the right place at the right time to get exactly what you need to help you attain your goal.

Find your inner strength, love without attachment, live without fear and understand that…

> *"Balance is knowing when to intend,*
> *When to have a goal and fight for it,*
> *And when to surrender, letting go of all expectations*
> *In full faith that the highest and best will happen."*

In the challenges you had to overcome, you can be an inspiration to others by sharing the lessons you have learned. Most people will agree that if you search really well, there is a gift that can be found in the pain. No matter how difficult your situation was, if you have used the pressure of those extreme circumstances to become a "precious diamond," there are people who need to hear your story. What lessons can you teach others who are facing the same situation? How can you encourage and motivate others? What expertise do you have that others can benefit from? How can you make a difference?

All of the authors in this book are sharing their lessons with you and now empower others with their experiences. You can do the same! Think about it—when you capture your message on paper, you can reach people you may never meet in person, you can touch the lives of people in countries you have never heard of, you can motivate someone to create the life he never thought possible . . . you can touch and inspire the world!

Have you ever thought about writing a book? Are you a coach, speaker or entrepreneur with an empowering message? It's time to get your book out of you and on paper! It's easy to let the world around you and your circumstances distract you from your intention to become an author. You have a uniqueness that will be lost if you don't share it. There never has been another you, nor will there ever be. If you don't capture your story, your experience and your life lessons, they may be lost forever. Plus, it is fun and fulfilling to make money by doing something that has a positive effect in other people's lives.

Take action now and email me at books@coauthorswanted.com to get your free audio, "Write, Inspire, Prosper," and discover how you can prosper by making a difference in the world.

"When life hands you lemons, make lemonade...
Write down the recipe and sell it!"

— ABOUT THE AUTHOR —

© NAOMI KING

Shamayah Sarrucco's passion is to help entrepreneurs share their empowering messages with the world. Shamayah is a gifted writer who incorporates her extensive business expertise in the books, blogs, and other marketing materials she writes for her clients. Shamayah is an in-demand speaker, available to speak for groups of business owners or students about "The Art of Intention" and "The Million Dollar Business Card – How to write your own book." She is the author of *Googlicious* and *You are a Precious Diamond*. Visit her website www.WorldClassWriting.com or email her at Books@worldclasswriting.com.

I Pray…

I pray, "Father, tell me."
He says, "Let it go."

I pray, "Father, I love him."
He says, "Focus on me."

I pray, "Father, I miss him."
He says, "My love will carry you."

I pray, "Father, show me the way."
He says, "Surrender your heart."

I pray, "Father, direct my steps."
He says, "Follow the path."

I pray, "Father, give me more faith."
He says, "Patience my child."

I pray, "Father, I love you."
He says, "Your heart's desires you will receive."

– Shamayah

Based on Isaiah 43:13, Jeremiah 10:23 and Psalms 145:16

CHAPTER 3

The Infinite Success Formula

Ramesh Kumar, MD

*"Keep your feet on the ground, your head in the clouds,
the stars in your eyes — and make your dream come true."*
— Vinutha Kumar

y medical practice was thriving; I was living my dream. I was seeing as many patients as I could fit in every day, and my life was filled with a richness that comes from making a difference in other people's lives. We owned and operated two very successful cancer centers that brought in several hundred thousand dollars a year. Everything seemed to be perfect. Little did I know how quickly everything would change.

One day, I began to notice that the income was dropping, despite the fact that business was still thriving. Before long, I was bringing in less than $2,000 a month, even though I was working 15 hours a day. My business partner brushed it off, saying it was due to having a ton of expenses, but as it turned out, he only said that to cover up the fact that profits were being stolen right from under my nose. When I requested an audit, he used his majority share in one of the two cancer centers to force me out of my own practice. I wound up practicing in a small town, but because his uncle was still in charge of billing, I was in debt for $600,000 before I knew it.

It was a complete reversal of everything I had known. I didn't know what to do—I felt so stunned, so *hopeless*. I was in debt for over half a million dollars. I didn't know anything about the business side of the practice; I knew how to treat patients, but anything beyond that was like a foreign language. I recall sitting at home, staring blankly at a wall, not knowing how I was going to provide for my family— I had no income and this huge mountain of debt. Worst of all, it forced me to leave my patients who had put their trust in me. One day, my little 7-year-old girl, Vinutha, came up to me to show me the story she had written. She said it was called "The Thief who Became King." That was my wake-up call—I realized I couldn't let that happen. I had to get in gear, had to change things. I had to turn my life around and get everything back on track.

When you don't have the money required to start your own business or get back on your feet after a setback, you have to become creative and resourceful. For instance, I wanted to start my own cancer center, but in order to do so, I needed to raise over 10 million dollars. Everyone told me that it was an impossible task. I took that as a challenge, and things just fell into place. Having the right partners, and with the support of several of my friends and family, we pulled it off!

Through all this, my patients stayed with me; despite the fact that it was a sacrifice for them to travel two hours, they refused to see another doctor, even if they were feeling sick.

Along the way to finding success and achieving my goals, I developed the Infinite Success Formula. It is a simple and scalable solution that can work for any person and company, in any situation.

The Infinite Success Formula has three basic ingredients.

1 **The Right You** – This means becoming the best person you can be. You want to fix your mind, nurture your body, and create an environment that is supportive. What do you need to improve? What skills do you need to learn? Keep learning and developing yourself—be a better person today than you were yesterday. Being "the right you" also means that you take good care of yourself physically, emotionally and spiritually. Make sure that you get enough sleep, so your body can recharge and you feel energized to take the required actions in order to achieve your goals. By eating the right foods, you give your body the nutrients it needs to stay fit and healthy. Live your passion and feed your mind with positive, empowering thoughts and information. This will give you the mental power to achieve the success you desire. Take the time to meditate and become silent. Dress nicely and create a pleasant environment for yourself. You will build your self-esteem and self-confidence to face the world, no matter what challenges you may face.

2 **The Right Knowledge** – You need specific knowledge pertaining to your industry and niche. You must be at the top of your game, or else you will lose credibility very fast. You have to be a master in your field. You also need general knowledge concerning all aspects of your business. You should have enough knowledge to be able have an intelligent discussion with the professionals around you who help you run your business, and be able to call them on their mistakes. In my case, the biggest mistake I had made was having no knowledge about the business of the health care industry. I only had specific knowledge as a medical doctor. It wasn't until I had learned the general knowledge as a business owner that I could take control of my life and achieve my goals, because I was no longer depending on somebody else.

Having the right knowledge is empowering, so never stop learning. Seek out people who have the expertise you need and don't be afraid to ask for help. Education never stops. Your brain is a muscle, always ready to be exercised, to be molded to take on more success-based behaviors. Never tell yourself, "I already know that." It will kill the flow of information to your brain. Instead, always keep yourself open to any opportunity to learn new skills or knowledge, even if it doesn't pertain to your field of expertise—you never know what two things might work together, no matter how unlikely or disparate they might seem. Keep asking yourself, "What don't I see?" The brain works best when you tease it with a question, sorting through its vast library to come up with an answer for your query.

3 **The Right Vehicle** – There are many ways to achieve success. There is not a right or a wrong way, as long as you have honesty and integrity. You have to decide what the right vehicle is for you. The vehicle you choose will determine the speed at which you will achieve your goals. Do you want to take a Concord jet, an airplane, or a ship to get to your destination? You can have a job and earn a couple thousand dollars a month, or you can become an entrepreneur and make a load of money. The choice is up to you. In my situation, I chose to go the route of putting together the most modern, state-of-the-art cancer center, comparable to any university-level hospital in the country.

Fueling Your Dreams

You need to ask yourself, "Why do I want this level of success?" Unless you have a big "why," you will get stuck. "Why" needs to be inspirational, deeply rooted, passionate. It needs to be about the people— that is the fuel for your jet. This propels your ideas and passion forward. For instance, if you just want to make a lot of money, it probably won't be enough to drive you, to fuel you to keep going. Go deep inside to figure out your "why." Otherwise, any small obstruction can take you out of the game. Your "why" must be so strong, so powerful, that the desire to achieve your goals is like gasping for your last breath of air. One of my mentors shared the following story with me.

Once upon a time, there was a young boy who wanted to learn how to succeed in life. He asked many people for their secrets, but they were unable to share anything with him that worked. Finally one day, he met a wise old man who agreed to mentor him. He said that if the boy wanted to learn the secret to success, he needed to meet him on the beach at 6:00 AM. The boy said that he didn't usually get up that early, but the old man insisted. So, the next morning, the boy dutifully arrived at the beach early in the morning. The sun was just beginning to rise, casting a dim grey light across the water. There were very few people there at that hour, so it was easy for him to pick out the form of his mentor standing at the shoreline. The old man noticed him as he approached and smiled, the wrinkles drawing tight over his face. He instructed the boy to wade out into the water with him. They made their way out, and the boy began to notice with alarm that the water was getting deeper and deeper. Soon, it was up to his chin, and the mentor told him to stop. He placed his hand on top of the boy's head—and suddenly, he pushed him down under the water. The boy struggled and flailed in an effort to get his head above water again, but the mentor's grip was strong. It seemed like an eternity that this went on, although it couldn't have been more than a minute or two. Finally, when the boy was nearly exhausted and almost completely drowned, the man's hold loosened and he came up to the surface, gasping for air. He looked up at the mentor with hurt and confusion in his eyes, demanding an explanation. The old man smiled kindly and told him to remember the sensation of drowning, of being so close to giving out that he would do *anything* for just one more breath. That was the key to success—he needed to look for it that desperately, praying and begging for it when there was no other alternative.

What is your "why?" Does it motivate you to fight for it as if you are fighting for your last breath of air? Are you willing to do whatever it takes? My "why" is to have a positive effect on young physicians who are clueless about the business side of our profession and prevent them from making costly mistakes.

Your Navigation Device

Another key to success is finding the right mentorship. Your mentors are your navigation device. They can guide you so that you won't get lost or go in the wrong direction—there is no need for detours if you are willing to listen to and learn from others. Find mentors who resonate with your ideals and vision. They can become your navigators, guiding you to success and allowing you to see what you may not see on your own. When all these things work together, you'll lift off with such momentum that nothing will be able to stop you.

If you are a physician or a health care provider and are ready to take your practice to the next level, let me be your mentor. Time and time again, I've come across physicians who are excellent doctors but are horrible at running a business, which unfortunately is NEVER taught in medical schools. As one who has suffered through catastrophic events in my own life, I have dedicated my life to helping you thrive in your business while you continue to serve your patients. You don't have to struggle or suffer financial disasters that could destroy your career and your family. Get your free copy of the eBook *The Secret of the Infinite Success Formula for Physicians and Health Care Providers* today by sending an email to Theinfinitesuccessformula@gmail.com.

— ABOUT THE AUTHOR —

Dr. Ramesh Kumar is a board-certified Radiation Oncologist and the co-founder of a multi-million dollar state-of-the-art Radiation Oncology cancer center in Florida. Apart from helping several thousand cancer patients lead richer lives, his passion is to empower physicians in the business aspect of medicine. Ramesh guides solo private practitioners who are starting in their medical offices or who are recovering from their medical business losses to create a prosperous practice. Ramesh can be reached at 772-293-0377. www.curingcancerofthemind.com

Winning the Money Game

K. Ryn Deitz

> *"Financial stress reduction is as much about being relaxed*
> *and happy as it is about making a lot of money.*
> *Ideally, you want to be making more money*
> *and having more fun on a daily basis."*
> – Chellie Campbell

*W*hat are your goals and dreams? Would you like to take the love of your life to the top of the Eiffel Tower in Paris? Do you want your children to go to the best college? Would you like to drive an Audi R8? Or to support your aging parents so they can retire? How would your life change if you earned $1,000/$2,500/$5,000 more a month? Or do you simply want to live debt free? Of course, achieving any of these dreams will make you happy, but what if you could be happier as you move toward your money goals, instead of having to wait until you have obtained them? Having more happiness right now is something that you can build into your money goals every step of the way.

When I first decided to move from "getting by" to making some "real money," I read *Rich Dad Poor Dad*. The book said I needed to change my thoughts, because rich people think differently about money than middle class people. Unfortunately, the book didn't talk about how to change my thoughts. So for years I struggled along, learning how to invest in real estate but having very conflicting thoughts and emotions about money. It was like driving a car with the parking brake on. The investing was going great, but life was sure hard! After four years of an improving financial situation mixed with emotional misery, I read Chellie Campbell's *The Wealthy Spirit* and learned about using affirmations, an amazingly powerful way to change my thinking about money. This worked so well, one coaching client hired me because I was the only person she knew who "lights up with happiness" when I talk about money.

Since then, I've learned many different ways to change what you think and believe about money. I am going to share five of them with you in this chapter.

Here are some of my favorite ways to build happiness as you achieve your money goals:

1 **Pick a money goal that has you laughing with delicious delight!** When I ask people about their money goals, I often hear things like, "Well, I have to get out of debt," and, "I ought to save more," and, "I need to make more money." Their tone of voice sounds as if someone is coming to drag them off into some horrible money dungeon until this dire situation is remedied.

So, here's a hint for all of you "money dungeon" people out there: If you pick a "have to" money goal, you are probably doomed — beaten before you start. Why? Because unless someone is standing over you with a stick, ready to beat you if you screw up, you are probably not going to be able to keep up the momentum long enough to reach this goal.

Instead, pick a money goal that has you all tingle-y with excitement and anticipation. Instead of saying things like, "I have to get out of debt," say, "When I pay off this credit card, I am going to take a whole day off and go to the beach (or the spa or fishing)!" And then, when you pay off the card, take that whole day!

This is similar to a martial artist breaking a board. In order to break a board with your fist, you don't aim at the board. Instead, you aim a couple of inches *beyond* the board. You picture your fist stopping *behind* the board, snap your punch. Your fist ends up exactly where you pictured it, several inches beyond where the board used to be. So picking a money goal that's fun, and one that is beyond your "have to" goal, means you achieve both goals and are happier along the way!

2 **Create a money metaphor that makes you smile!** Something that always amazes me is how negative people seem to be about the whole idea of money! Mainstream U.S. culture seems totally fixated on being serious about money – that earning money and managing it is hard, dull work. It's almost Victorian. Pain, suffering, and powerlessness. Stifling, dull, boring, frustrating! Media money people look intense, and their energy seems to be either frantic with anxiety, or very heavy with grave (self?) importance.

Yuck! Who needs that? Instead, choose a way to think about money that creates happiness and joy for you. Some metaphors I've used at one time or another and loved have been:

Gardening – Planting investment seeds and watching them grow.

Football – Needing a good offensive to get money, and a good defense to protect what I've got.

Dog Training – Telling my money to "Sit! Stay!" instead of wandering off goodness knows where!

Basically, you want to pick money metaphors that move you into a light, friendly, *fun* frame of mind. This means you are more likely to think about money in ways that open you up to possibilities. One of the reasons I smile when I think about money is that it is now one of my best friends.

3 **Notice and welcome the obstacles.** What is preventing your progress? A quick check is to set a mini-goal, something that will get you about one step closer to your money goal. Write this mini-money goal down in your planner. Flip ahead one week and schedule a check-in day and time approximately one week after you assigned yourself this task. When you get to the check-in appointment, did you accomplish the task? If not, then set that same goal and set up the check-in appointment yet another week ahead. Then once the second week is over, check on yourself. Have you accomplished the task yet?

If the answer is still no, that is a good indication that something in your life is blocking you; something is keeping you from completing that task. This is great (although it can be very annoying at the time). You have now pin-pointed a block, and once you have dealt with it, you will be able to move much more quickly toward your goal!

An example of this comes from one of my clients who had earned some fabulous commissions. Yet, she didn't save or invest any of that money, and so when times got tough, she didn't have much to fall back on. As we explored what might have created this painful pattern, she blurted out, "But I don't want to be rich!" The word rich, it turns out, brought up very negative emotions for her. And so she avoided "being rich" by making sure she never kept any of her money! Not wanting to "be rich" was a major block in her path toward reaching her money goals, a block that had impeded her progress for years! Yet, once we identified the problem, she was able to release the old, unhelpful belief about being rich and get back on the path to meeting her money goal.

4 **Show some respect!** It's important to honor money with your words and actions. You're now thinking of money in a positive way, you've got a money metaphor that makes you smile, and money is one of your absolute best friends. Would you expect someone to stay your best friend

long if you said disrespectful things about him to other people? There are many things we commonly say that are disrespectful of money and of people who have a lot of it (e.g.; cold, hard cash; filthy rich). An easy way to counter these negative money thoughts and sayings is to replace them with positive money thoughts and statements called affirmations. If you would like a free list of my 15 favorite money affirmations, and instructions on how to use them, go to www.thinkrichbehappy.com.

5   **Celebrate every win, big and small!** Finally, celebrate every win, big and small. You've got a new money metaphor? Woo hoo! That's a win! Celebrate it! You went to a store, made purchases and stayed on budget? Woo hoo! Definitely a win! You made your last car payment, renegotiated your interest rate, made a sale, filed your LLC forms? Yay! All wins.

Celebration is a habit. When you develop it, every day becomes full of goals achieved and all money becomes happy money. If you wait, only celebrating your big wins, you get out of practice and often have difficulty truly enjoying your big win. So celebrate all along the way. Plus, celebrating all along the way is great for helping you learn to celebrate creatively, so that you experience that quick jolt of joy without spending a lot of money or time or calories.

One of my favorite celebrations is something I developed spontaneously. One day I earned a great big commission, and I was just so full of happiness that I grabbed my stone frog and hopped it up and down the fireplace mantle. Celebration born! This frog is now my "sales frog." It sits by my desk, and when someone buys one of my products or services directly from me, I laugh and jump "sales frog" around on the desk. Silly, yes. And fun! So create a few celebrations of your own, and then go looking for wins to celebrate!

Have you figured out what's missing from your money vision? Is it full of celebration, joy and happiness? Does it contain lots of opportunities for fun and lightheartedness? If not, you can fix that! Take time right now and:

1. Pick a money goal that has you laughing with delicious delight!
2. Create a money metaphor that makes you smile!
3. Welcome the obstacles!
4. Show some respect!
5. Celebrate every win, big and small!

One of my money goals is to be happy with my money every single day of my life! And now that I know and practice the techniques listed above, I have truly stepped into that vision! Loving both the journey and the reaching of money goals is what I do. I work with you to identify and overcome whatever is blocking you on your journey toward your money goal. As a money coach, I don't just hand you a map and send you on your way. I actually walk the territory of your personal journey with you, and help you overcome the obstacles that stand between you and your goal.

— ABOUT THE AUTHOR —

© Julie Jay Photography

K. Ryn Deitz, Ph.D. is a Certified Financial Stress Reduction (R) Coach and CEO of Rocky Mountain Wealthy Spirit. RMWS specializes in working with you to develop the thoughts, the actions, and the focus that will ultimately result in you achieving your money goals so that you can live the life you really want. When she is not speaking, coaching and consulting, Dr. Ryn practices yoga, real estate investing, horseback riding, and enjoying life. For more information on her groundbreaking systems, visit www.RockyMtnWealthySpirit.com or call 303.494.5842.

CHAPTER 5

Awaken Your Full Potential

Jane Ann Covington

"Live in terms of your strong points. Magnify them.
Let your weaknesses shrivel up and die
from lack of nourishment."
– William Young Elliott

Whether you're a member of the C-suite, leading your own company, or working your way up the ladder, do you sometimes feel anxious or stressed out thinking that others might discover your vulnerabilities? Leaders frequently have to act as though they are invulnerable, even when they haven't figured it all out. Truth is, we're all vulnerable from time to time.

Emotional and social intelligence, as pointed out in Daniel Goleman's writings, are the most reliable predictors for your success. Brain-Based Learning Expert Eric Jensen reports that how we behave emotionally as adults was programmed into us by age 6 and the majority of that by age 3, as well as during our pre-teen years. So we unconsciously recreate these patterns over and over again throughout our lifetime. Unless we become aware of our patterns and intentionally choose to learn new options, we remain in a cycle that holds us back. To evolve successfully, objective feedback from an outside party or team of experienced individuals is required.

Goleman asserts that Emotional Intelligence (EQ) is a significantly higher predictor of success than the Intelligence Quotient (IQ). Naturally, being skilled at your profession is critical, but to get along and influence others you need both high emotional (EQ) and social (SQ) intelligence.

Environment also makes a huge impact on us and helps determine our potential success or failure. Perhaps you were fortunate enough to have had a friend, teacher, family member, boss, associate or mentor who helped you learn ways of effectively interacting with others. Yet, rarely is anyone raised in an atmosphere—at home, school, or work—where emotional and social intelligence was effectively modeled. And as importantly, you were not taught how to interact with yourself in a way that allowed you to discover what is possible for you to live a truly fulfilled, successful, and stress-free life.

Being human isn't easy. We are often blinded to what's truly possible for us or others. Your ability to be objective is often the illusion—the block. Top leaders understand that you must ask for feedback and help to become more objective, to reach your full potential, and help others along the way. This is an important mark of true leadership in today's environment—to become more diplomatic, creative, sophisticated, patient, yet proactive, effective in ways of thinking, believing, communicating, and behaving. We are all models for others, including our children and cohorts.

With guidance and feedback (perhaps just the right coach), you can expand to improve your chances for massive success. Even the most gifted and successful individuals, leaders and athletes realize the value of a really good coach.

Here are some action tips for moving forward that work!

1. **Appreciate yourself.** Everyone has unique gifts and sometimes under developed talents to share. Let go of the habit of comparing yourself to others, or criticizing yourself and others. Having an MBA or Ph.D.

isn't always the answer. Your job is to learn and be your personal best. You will be amazed at what you can achieve. You will have to work for it, but it will build your confidence. Regardless of your background, you will be able to do great things. Internal messages that were often learned unconsciously at a very early age do not have to be the continuing pattern or truth about your unique, real capabilities.

2 **Transform old programs.** Doing the same thing over and over again and expecting different results is the definition of insanity. Yet, most people live at that level (even those who become financially successful, at times). But times are *always* changing. Success demands that we must be flexible, aware, and have greater choice in our responses to our customers, employees, economy, family members, and self.

We all come with a body and brain, but without an instruction booklet. Neuroscience has come a long way. Knowing now that the brain is teachable and trainable, you *can, with help,* change your responses and behaviors to move beyond unconscious blocks, habits and patterns that no longer serve you—and probably never did.

3 **Find the right environment.** Your environment makes a huge difference in who you become and what you believe about yourself. Try visiting new environments where a whole new world of possibilities may open up for you. Get out and meet new people that are in alignment with where you want to go in life!

4 **Surround yourself with great people.** Learning from others, or hiring people smarter than you, is still a good idea. Caring, trustworthy, positive, smart, resourceful, successful role models or mentors are invaluable and awaken new leadership possibilities within. We've all had tough times. You may be going through one right now. In those tough times, it's the inner you and the people around you that will

help you make it through. Truly, no one is an island. Remember, successful people ask for help when they need it. Go towards people who encourage, challenge, and help bring out the best in you.

5   **Expect success!** True success has a wholeness to it. Money alone doesn't create success if you have no peace, love, freedom or joy within yourself or in the world around you. Always remember that your path is unique. What's right for others may not be your path. Your definition of success may also be unique.

Of course, you will find that rarely does anyone have a straight path. Just learn everything you can along the way. Success can come in ordinary and unique ways. Having an MBA or a Ph.D. in Economics doesn't guarantee you will succeed, but it won't hurt you, either, as long as you have healthy Emotional and Social Intelligence to go along with it.

My clients and years of experience in helping people take action to create a better life have taught me that as objective as we all would like to think we are, changing ones mindset typically takes work and requires outside professional help in assisting you to quickly overcome blocks, allowing you to flourish. Life takes patience and persistence... life isn't linear and you may get distracted and stuck in a rut along the way. You can exchange the rut for your true path.

What are you waiting for? "Making it to the top" doesn't always make you feel great about yourself. You may still believe that you are not good enough in some way. You may be super stressed, or your relationships with those around you may be unhappy. Are you waiting for "them" or the world to change? That may or may not happen anytime soon. But you can help by changing yourself. Don't wait any longer to be more effective, loved and appreciated. Everyone who truly wants to feel and be successful eventually must go inward to release unwanted, unhelpful patterns and replace the inner programming with positive, healthy IQ, EQ, and SQ to assure your greater wholeness, peace and true success.

How to get started? Request your free audio *14 Minute Chill* at www.JaneAnnCovington.com/bookspecial. It's up to you to start making your life more peaceful and meaningful. You were put here to do good things—to bring your unique, special talents and abilities to the world in business, personal, social, and other dynamic ways. Seek and find the help you need. You can develop yourself into a dynamic force for good and have a satisfying, prosperous, happy life! Your full potential self awaits its awakening within you.

Best wishes to you and thank goodness you are among us!

Jane Ann Covington

"You Can Awaken Your Full Potential Highest Self…"
~Jane Ann Covington

— ABOUT THE AUTHOR —

Jane Ann Covington's expertise is to help people discover their full potential self. Her practical, confidential, unique coaching, education and consulting hypnotherapy methodology is an effective, results-oriented, customized program derived from 35 years of training and experience, including a B.A. in Developmental Psychology and as a Registered Behavioral Therapist. She skillfully helps clients become free to act according to current conditions instead of react to past patterns. Author, inspirational speaker, and workshop trainer, she is also the founder and director of Center for Developing Mastery. www.JaneAnnCovington.com

CHAPTER 6

Building a Mindful Business

Violetta Terpeluk

> *"Successful people don't leave things to chance —*
> *they create their lives actively."*
> – Michael Gerber

When you go on a road trip, do you just get in your car and start driving? You may be excited to see the sights of your destination, but without a plan, a roadmap and gas in your car, chances are you will never get there. Your trip will require proper planning and preparation in case something unexpected happens. You can't just take off in hopes that you will miraculously arrive at your desired location, yet that is how most people run their business. You want your business to provide you with the lifestyle you want to live now and in the long run. Like the road trip, planning and a well-thought-out roadmap are key.

How do you create a mindful business? There are four key points to keep in mind:

1) Begin with the end in mind
2) Build and grow from the inside out
3) Prepare for the unexpected
4) Stay on track

1 **Begin with the end in mind.** It is critical that you spend time soul searching. It will help you find clarity on what your true purpose in life is and what you personally want to get out of life. So before you decide on your goals and numbers, ask yourself the following questions:

- ☆ What do I really want to accomplish in my life?
- ☆ What is my purpose or my ultimate life game?
- ☆ What are my values?
- ☆ When I am on my death bed, what do I see myself having done?
- ☆ What lifestyle do I want to live?
- ☆ When do I want to retire?
- ☆ What is my business exit plan?

These questions are important to think about when you go on a road trip. You need to map out where you want to go in your life and plan how to get there. Knowing how you want to exit your business will determine your actions today, and it will give you clarity on how to build and grow your company.

What is the ultimate goal for your business? Do you want to be the owner and have somebody else run the company for you? Or do you want to sell it? A clear business exit plan will show how much money you will need to live the lifestyle you envision, and what you have to do to bridge the gap of where you are today and where you want to be. It also has to show how much you will need to accumulate on a yearly basis. As your life evolves, your goal may change. Take the time to sit down and make the needed adjustments to your plan.

2 **Build and grow from the inside out.** Soul searching will also help you identify your values. Your values must represent who you are and what your motive in life is. Once you are clear on your values, you set the context for your business. Your business has to be in alignment with who you are.

Be clear on your personal goals first—as an individual or as a family—because this will allow you to plan your business from the inside out. When you know what lifestyle you want to live, now and in the future, you can create a plan for your company to help you achieve that. You may want to be financially independent by a certain age, support your parents financially, or take several trips a year. Your personal goals should always come before your business goals. When you don't set the right priorities and instead make your business more important than yourself, you won't be happy. But when you intertwine your personal aspirations with those for your business, you will pave your road to success.

Expand the context of your goals by connecting them with your deeper motivations and desires. Suppose you want to pay for your children's education. The first step is to decide how much money you need and what your yearly revenue has to be. You break it down to a monthly goal—how many new clients do you need each month to reach your goal? And then you determine what this really means in your life: "One new client a month will mean x amount in my college fund for my kids." Isn't that more meaningful than a plain dollar amount as your monthly goal? Connect your passion and your numbers—it will drive you and give you power!

Designing your business from the inside out also means that you grow mindfully. Instead of just setting a goal of how much money you want to make, make a conscious choice of the kind of people you want to do business with and attract clients you enjoy working with.

As you grow your company, you want to keep your exit strategy in mind. Knowing your destination and having a road map will help you decide which route to take. Keep in mind that there are 3 ways a business owner can get paid:

1) When you work in your business, you need to pay yourself a salary.

2) You can get a share of the profit or a bonus, based on the performance of the company.

3) You can receive a lump sum of money all at once or a passive income on a regular basis when you step away, because of the equity you built in the business.

When your plan is to sell your company, your strategy for growth may be different than the one you'll use with the objective of having your children take over for you when you decide to retire.

3 **Prepare for the unexpected.** Life is full of unforeseen events, and you have to be prepared for them. You need to prepare for the certainty of uncertainty. What if something happens to you and you become disabled, or you can't work anymore? How will you be able to provide for your family? Do you have a backup plan? What if you die unexpectedly? Can your business run without you? Most of us think that those things won't happen to us, but they forget that accidents do happen every day.

It is critical that you take the time to prepare for the unexpected. It may never happen, but isn't it much better to be prepared than to have an emergency and not have your emergency plan in place? Just like you have a spare tire in your trunk, you need to have a backup plan in case you get sick, injured or die unexpectedly.

4 **Stay on track.** Your business evolves, and so does your life. Allow flexibility in order to adjust your journey and your destination, because even your exit plan can change. Soul searching is not a one-time process. Your purpose and passion can change over time. Your situation and your family needs can change. If the unexpected happens, you may have to set new goals and adjust your plan. Even though you need to be flexible, be careful that you don't make your

goals a moving target by changing them all the time. There is a delicate balance between staying on track and being flexible.

When you have somebody on your team as your advisor, you will have somebody that can hold you accountable, provide you with objective opinions, help you track your progress, as well as guide you in creating and adjusting your plans. You can get so wrapped up running your business that you may forget to look at all the different aspects that come with building a mindful business.

In summary, building a mindful business means creating your lifestyle in alignment with your personal values and dreams—the lifestyle that makes you happy. Knowing the end you have in mind will determine your business strategy and your daily activities. In order to succeed in achieving your goals, you need to consciously map out your plan. Be clear on your numbers. Know how you are going to get from where you are today to where you want to be. And be prepared for the unexpected. This can be a challenge to do on your own. But one day, it could be too late—you could get injured and think, "If only I had protected myself and my family." Or you could start contemplating your retirement, but realize you should have started planning 10 years sooner. Don't let that happen to you. It is my passion to help successful business owners like you design their business to serve the lifestyle they desire now and in the future. Contact me to schedule your complimentary strategy session.

— ABOUT THE AUTHOR —

Violetta Sit Terpeluk is a Certified Financial Planner® practitioner, a business financial advisor and a franchise owner with one of the largest financial planning companies in the nation. She has her MBA in Corporate Strategy from the University of Michigan Ross School of Business and was a management consultant with PricewaterhouseCoopers. Violetta's passion is to help successful small business owners design, create and monitor their financial plan for their life and business by developing wealth preservation, retirement income, business succession and tax planning strategies.   http://www.ameripriseadvisors.com/violetta.s.terpeluk, violetta.s.terpeluk@ampf.com, 916.787.9988

CHAPTER 7

Soul-Powered Goals:
Set Yourself on Fire!

Annette Marie Pieper

*"In your life's defining moments there are two
choices — you either step forward in faith and power
or you step backward into fear."*
— James Arthur Ray

*A*fter 21 years of marriage, it had broken down beyond repair. I had always dreamed of having a passionate relationship with my spouse. I had dreamed of being a positive role model of success for my children, showing them how wonderful life can be. My life had not turned out that way; my reality was far from my dreams. There was absolutely no sense of peace or stability. I was miserable, but I stayed anyway. In 2009 I made the decision several times to leave my husband, yet nothing changed. I was still there, trapped in my own fear.

Looking back, it's clear that making a decision is not enough. You need to set yourself on fire to make a change and achieve your goals! We all have dreams or a vision of what we want our lives to look like, but what do you do when your reality is miles apart from your vision? What do you do when you feel miserable? Do you stay anyway?

Let me share with you the 10 steps—my Soul-Powered Goal Process—that transformed my life.

1 **Create Your Success Blueprint.** What is the ultimate outcome that you want to achieve? Many times, we focus on getting out of our current situation. When we are in this frame of mind, our goal may be, "I want to quit this job," or, "I want to lose weight." These are ineffective statements and move us away from our real goals. When we identify what we do want, it pulls us forward. It's the fuel that keeps us fired up to keep moving. Examples might be, "I want to have a fit and healthy 130-pound body," or, "I want to work in an environment that inspires me." Many times when we focus on what moves us away from our deepest desires, we get caught up in fear and doubt. Moving towards something we passionately want is much more energizing and inspiring.

When I met with my Mastermind group in beautiful Lake Oswego, Oregon, the first weekend of August in 2009, we stayed in a home right at the end of a canal that flowed into the lake—it was absolutely peaceful. We were surrounded by water, colorful flowers, big shady trees and greenery. Sharing this awe-inspiring environment with like-minded people helped me to create my blueprint.

I have a BIG vision for who I want to be in the world. The chaos in my marriage was creating a big barrier to the level of success I desired. The group made me see that as long as I allowed myself to feel victimized by my circumstances, my dreams would never become a reality. Two days later, I informed my husband of my decision to leave. With the goal achievement blueprint I had crafted, I set myself on fire.

2 **Paint Your Dream.** Write out what it will look like and feel like when you achieve the outcome you desire. Use colorful, emotional words to describe your feelings. Paint a picture with your words. When Vincent Van Gogh was asked how he was able to paint his amazing pictures, he said, "I dream my painting, then I paint my dream." Paint your dream or goal with your words. Once you have it on paper, close your eyes and visualize the outcome. Be in the picture, not just observing you in the picture. Feel the feelings. Bring in colors, shapes, tastes, sounds, smells and textures. Make it as vivid as possible. Spend time visualizing your outcome at least twice a day. Visualize before you fall asleep, then the unconscious mind which never sleeps can work on it while the conscious mind sleeps. Visualize it again first thing in the morning, to engage both the conscious and the unconscious mind to help in the creation process.

3 **Know Your Big "Why."** Why do you want to achieve your goal? You might say something like, "I want to make more money," "I want to weigh 130 pounds," or "I want a new relationship." Great, but do those really inspire you and connect you to your emotions and feelings? What does making more money give you? Do you get freedom, the ability to spend more time with your family, travel the world or spend more time golfing with your friends?

When I separated from my husband, my big "why" was to experience inner peace, live in a peaceful environment, and have healthy, happy kids. I wanted to be a positive role model of joy and success for my children so they could create a more empowered future for themselves. Your big WHY must create an emotional response that excites you and connects you with your vision. Whatever works for you is best. You'll know when you have it by the way you feel. It's energizing!

4 **Give It a Name.** Have you ever noticed how the military or a non-profit organization gives a project or a military operation a name? Names such as "Project Hope" or "Operation Desert Storm" are some

you may be familiar with. Why do they do that? It gives the project POWER! It is an organizing principle that rallies everyone together, inspires them to reach for what they can accomplish, keeps them focused on a common goal and energizes them through the collective energy of working for a greater cause. There is power in the name. It is no longer a goal, it's a quest —a journey to a destination.

When I left my husband, I named my goal "Operation Harvest Moon." I set the goal of moving within two months to coincide with the full Harvest Moon, and I planned to have a party to celebrate. Give your goal a powerful name that represents the end results or the timeframe that you have set. Get silly or be serious, just make it inspiring!

5 **Create Your Master Plan.** Imagine a line in front of you, from where you are now to the goal you want to achieve. Map it out on the floor. Now step into the future place of your goal and bring up the vision you created earlier. Then, looking back to your starting point, what steps did you take to get to your goal? Pay attention to what comes to mind and get it down on paper. This way you can organize the steps and make any adjustments that you need to as you create your goal plan. Also, what are the potential obstacles that you may encounter along the way? When you map them out, you can decide in advance how you will deal with them if they show up and you are less likely to be knocked off your game.

6 **Decide on a Timeframe.** It's critical to have a timeframe in mind for your goals. When we give a deadline for our goals, it creates a sense of urgency. How long will it realistically take to reach your goal? Now stretch yourself a little to create that sense of urgency. A sense of urgency provides a pull and gets us out of our comfort zones and moving in a forward direction.

7 **Build Confidence.** Create an affirmation to support your goal such as, "Everything in my life flows easily and effortlessly to support my desired outcome." Affirmations engage the unconscious mind. Think of a computer. Your brain is the hardware, your mind is the operating system and affirmations are the software programs that you install. Write your affirmations on post-it notes or 3x5 cards and post them where you can read them several times every day. Repeat them over and over again like a mantra, as you visualize.

8 **Make a Mind Map.** We have a conscious and an unconscious mind. The conscious mind only represents about 10% of our mind. The other 90% is our unconscious mind. It's time to begin your reconditioning program. The unconscious mind is not linear. It sees in pictures, so a mind map is a very powerful tool to create an image that engages this part of our mind. (Get your mind map download at www.visiontorealitytraining.com/mindmap). I prefer to draw my mind maps using colored markers. Drawing and writing are kinesthetic activities that engage the unconscious mind. The unconscious mind also responds to colors, as well.

9 **Pick Music to Ignite Your Soul Fire.** Music connects us to our emotions and produces a feeling in our bodies. Let the music inspire the thoughts, emotions and feelings to fuel the process. When I started Operation Harvest Moon, I picked "The Time of My Life," by David Cook. I would listen to the song as I visualized my Harvest Moon Party. When I heard the song, it would remind me of where I was going rather than the heartache I was experiencing. I would vividly envision myself in the scenario that the song describes, standing at the edge of a desert cliff looking out over the horizon and feeling the sun pouring over my face.

Pick a Power Song that makes your heart sing with joy, that ignites the Soul Fire within and keeps fueling the fire with inspiration.

10 **Get Support and De-clutter.** It's critical to have support. You will run into many obstacles, such as getting stuck in limiting beliefs, thought patterns and emotions as you work to achieve your goals. Hire a coach, find an accountability partner and get some support for your journey. Contact me if you are interested in having me as a support partner. I would never have achieved my goals without the support of my Mastermind group, coaches and accountability partners. Be sure you have some sort of accountability system in place to keep you on track when distractions and obstacles come along.

We must clean up our lives in order to reach the level of success we desire. We have to clean up our mindset, get rid of beliefs that are no longer serving us, get help for emotional issues we may be having, let go of excess physical weight and poor dietary habits, and clean up clutter and chaos in our physical environment. There are times when we have bigger messes to clean up, such as dysfunctional relationships, letting go of negative people, leaving negative work environments, getting out of debt and other big barriers.

Clutter can create roadblocks that prevent you from achieving your goals.

Lights, Camera, Action!

You've mapped out your goal. You've laid out the details, now what? Get into action! Take the first step that you have outlined, then the next one. Create a daily plan of action. Even the best laid plans will not come about without big action. Remember to get your support system in place and enjoy the process. Celebrate all the little steps along the way and plan a big celebration of your goal success. Celebration gives us the momentum to keep pushing on.

By applying my Soul-Powered Goal Process, I have tripled my business income; I am speaking and conducting professional trainings through live events and teleseminars. Most importantly, my family is thriving. I have created a much more peaceful home environment and have great relationships with my kids and my former husband.

I want to give you a gift for reading this book and to support you on your Soul-Powered journey. Go to www.VisionToRealityTraining.com/goalbook to receive a free audio instruction download and mind map template ($97 Value). I would love to hear your stories of success. Feel free to email me your success stories or ask questions at vision@AnnettePieper.com.

— ABOUT THE AUTHOR —

Annette Marie Pieper, The Soul Power Coach, transforms lives by guiding people out of self-sabotaging habits, limiting beliefs and thought patterns and teaches them to unleash their inner power. Annette coaches and mentors hundreds of individuals each year as she weaves together a variety of personal, business and wealth development tools to support each individual's unique journey to create and achieve their goals. www.VisionToRealityTraining.com

PASSION.

Ignite the fire of your soul and create a better life — not only for you, but also for those around you. Make a difference by sharing your story or expertise with others. Email books@coauthorswanted.com to discover how you can "Write, Inspire & Prosper," or to share how you have enjoyed this book.

CHAPTER 8

Turn Your Dreams Into Reality!

Dr. Will Fishkin

> *"The victory of success is half won when one gains the habit of setting goals and achieving them. Even the most tedious chore will become endurable as you parade through each day convinced that every task, no matter how menial or boring, brings you closer to fulfilling your dreams."*
>
> – Og Mandino

*M*y hands were sweaty and my stomach was growling. I had never been so nervous in my life! Standing backstage, waiting for the call to step onto the platform. . . this was the moment that I had waited for for so many years, and now that it was here, I didn't know if I would survive. Suddenly I heard the announcement, "Let me introduce to you the winner of the National Referral Marketing Competition of 2011, Dr. William Fishkin!!!" There was a thunderous sound of applause! The bright lights shining in my face prevented me from seeing the audience, but there had to be thousands of people. As I got ready to speak, I heard someone ask, "Will, are you ready?" In a split second, I woke up and realized that I had been daydreaming. It was my turn to get on stage during a workshop. Although this was not exactly how I had dreamed it, everyone applauded.

How do you go from daydreaming to making your dreams your reality? Follow these these 7 Success Steps Secrets:

1 **Identify your purpose & create an inspiring vision.** Your purpose and vision will motivate you to take the next step. It is important that you understand the distinction between vision and purpose. Your vision is how you see yourself in the future, without any regard to reality. Your vision statement comprises the words you use to describe the picture of how you see yourself in the future, so that you can keep your vision alive in your consciousness. Your purpose describes WHY you do what you do. Your purpose statement is what your inner voice says to you, which keeps you in touch with why you do what you do and why you are inspired to do it. I have created a powerful process that can help you create a new vision and a powerful purpose for your life. You can download this teleseminar and the workbook by going to the following website: http://www.makingmarketingmiracles.com/purpose

2 **Make a bold declaration of your intention.** You must declare your intention publicly. Declaring your intention when you are home by yourself doesn't count. Declare it around people who will hold you accountable. It would be even better to ask them to hold you accountable.

3 **Create a step-by-step plan.** The best way to create a powerful plan is to start with the END RESULT you want to achieve and then work backwards, step by step, identifying all of the major parts of the process that you need to accomplish along the way.

4 **Take immediate action to get started.** After you have written down your plan step by step, you must do one more thing — you must

take ACTION! Implement the first step of your plan and get started. You cannot wait until tomorrow or next week or when you will have the time or when it is convenient. You must take immediate ACTION!

"Procrastination is the bad habit of putting off until the day after tomorrow what should have been done the day before yesterday."
— Napoleon Hill

Once I had created my plan for "The Ultimate Referral Marketing Program," I ran the risk of becoming overwhelmed by this huge goal. So what I did was I took some IMMEDIATE ACTION and started to implement some of the parts of my plan that I could. For example, I scheduled the dates of the teleseminars (which were months away) and I set up the free conference call lines for these teleseminars. Although they would take place way in the future, taking immediate action on my plan made it more real and helped me to visualize it happening. When you create your plan, you can take some immediate action toward achieving your goals, too!

5 **Regularly review your outcomes and adjust your plan, if needed.** This is another key step in the process of achieving your goals and it is critical. On a regular basis, you must take time to look at your overall plan. Just as a pilot is constantly monitoring and reviewing the flight plan to see if the plane is still on course, you need to assess your progress and check to see if you are still on track. It can be that you need to adjust your plan or your timeline in order to get the end result you desire.

There may be times when you are making amazing progress and then, out of nowhere, you suddenly feel totally overwhelmed. When this happens, go back to step 1 and reconnect with your purpose and vision.

This will re-inspire you and can help you to re-assess your plan, your approach and your options. From there, you can make the course corrections needed to proceed powerfully once again!

6 **Stay committed to the end result.** Keep taking action and stay committed to the end result, no matter what. It is important that you stay focused on your plan and implement every part of it. Put a copy of your purpose, vision, goals and your plan in different places — in your office, your house or make it a wallpaper on your computer.

Sometimes an opportunity can open up that gets you on the fast track to achieving your goal. Pay attention to these opportunities. Be ready so you can take action quickly when the opportunity presents itself. This happened to me. . .

In January, I received Dan Kennedy's newsletter with a form that said, "Enter to win the 2011 Referral Marketing Program of the Year Award!" This was it! I could enter this contest and win this award. It would give me a national presence which I could use to help small business owners all over the country! I collected all of the referral marketing strategies I had applied to my chiropractic practices and added the key elements of my "Creating Your Ultimate Referral Marketing Program," put it all on a CD and sent it in before the deadline. Months of waiting went by. I visualized myself receiving the award and, as I shared earlier, daydreamed about it. Then, on July 14, 2011, I got this email:

To: Dr. William Fishkin (drwillf@pacbell.net)
From: Sherri (sherri@dankennedy.com)

Subject: You have won the 2011 Referral Marketing Contest!

I could not believe my eyes! Whooo-hoo! I did it! By focusing on my goal, powerful planning, taking action, staying committed, never quitting—and stepping back at times to look at the bigger picture: my vision—I had won the award!

7 **Celebrate your wins!** Acknowledge your progress every day and celebrate your wins! This is an important lesson that Tony Robbins taught me. One of the great problems with goal setting is that we wait until we achieve the goal to acknowledge what we have done and celebrate. So, the best way to continue to keep your energy level high toward achieving your goals is, on a daily basis, review your day, acknowledge where you have made progress in the steps and details of your plan and celebrate it! Tell yourself, "Good job!" and take in that you have gotten closer to achieving your goal.

If you follow these 7 simple steps you will accomplish your goals. . . you will turn your dreams into reality. You must be disciplined and continually revisit your vision to see yourself having achieved your goals and revisit your purpose so you will be inspired. You must have people, or at least one person, who know what you are up to and will hold you accountable to what you declare you are committed to doing. Then you make a plan and you put it into action. As you regularly review what you have accomplished, so far, and look at where you are headed, you make the adjustments and changes that you need to in order to be heading right toward your goals. Then, as you stay committed to your end result and regularly celebrate your progress, one day you will be celebrating the achievement of your goals. You have turned your dreams into reality!

As a Referral Marketing Expert, I teach business owners to nurture the relationships with their existing clients and business and professional associates by generating goodwill and creating lots of "raving fans." The best way that I can help you prepare for developing your own Ultimate Referral Marketing Program is by making sure you have an exciting vision and a purpose. As my gift to you to get you started on that path, you can download my Teleseminar, transcript and workbook on Creating an Exciting Vision and Powerful Purpose for your Business!

Go to: www.makingmarketingmiracles.com/purpose to get your FREE mp3 and transcript! If I can be of further help to you on your journey to success, email me at drfishkin@gmail.com and I will respond! I would love to communicate with you.

— ABOUT THE AUTHOR —

 Dr. Will Fishkin has been an expert in referral marketing for over 30 years, marketing his chiropractic business in Oakland and San Francisco for 20 years. He coaches chiropractors and other professionals in creating their Referral Marketing Programs for their businesses and is a speaker on marketing for professional organizations. He was featured on Russell Brunson's Successetc.com website with his award-winning Referral Marketing Program. He adores his wife, Janet, his daughters, Sara and Ariel Rose, and his two dogs. Dr. Will Fishkin's websites are: www.makingmarketingmiracles.com and www.drwillfishkin.com.

CHAPTER 9

Focus on Your Master Goal for Maximum Impact

Cliff Slaten

> *"You can change your entire life by changing the order of priority and importance of your goals."*
> – Brian Tracy

*I*t was the first of January. Like many, it was time to assess my old resolutions and goals and work on mapping out a plan for bringing my new ones to fruition. However, something wasn't adding up for me. The large tax practice I had worked so hard to build wasn't providing me with the financial security I thought it would. Another new year rolled around, and I noticed this trend had become an annual pattern of disappointment. Even though I had acquired ten tax practices, six tax preparers and serviced over 3500 clients, something wasn't adding up and it left me dead broke, wondering how I'd pay my bills. What was missing?

If you're concerned about earning enough money to live the life you've dreamed about, then go back and analyze what you've been doing. Ask yourself, what's missing?

In my case, the goal should have been centered on having consistent and reliable income all year round and not just during the months when taxes needed to be filed. That flawed plan didn't weigh in the impact of using seasonal income to cover twelve months of operating expenses. I was headed in the wrong direction.

One lesson this kind of situation teaches is that it's okay to change your direction when you realize things are headed the wrong way. Part of success is learning from mistakes and being flexible enough to make changes. My wife, Terrie, says, "If you want to reach your destination quickly, take the fastest route." When there are red flags encouraging you to make vital business changes, be ready to formulate an analysis and don't hesitate to make those changes.

Consider Your Ultimate Destination

To be able to take the proper steps in the right direction, you have to consider your ultimate destination. Have you created a plan for how you will arrive at that destination? If so, have you established the steps required to get you there? As an example, here are the steps you might take to achieve financial independence:

☆ Establish your starting point – where you are now.

☆ Decide on your end point – where you want to be.

☆ Determine your obstacles – what stands in your way.

☆ List your action steps, in order of importance, for overcoming those obstacles. These are your goals.

☆ Isolate the one goal which, if achieved, will have the greatest impact on accomplishing your objective. This is your Master Goal.

☆ Set a deadline for your Master Goal.

☆ Emulate success. How are other people like you achieving their goals? Analyze what they are doing, then use a similar approach.

Your Master Goal is almost always a powerful financial goal. This is what will lead you towards financial independence and provide you with the means to live the life of your dreams. Having a solid sense of where you want your business to ultimately go is going to help you get a better idea of what you need to do to get your business to that point. You'll begin to look for other businesses with a like model and will begin to analyze what makes their model work so well.

I chose to emulate successful financial advisors by hiring coaches, attending conventions and networking with my peers. Along the way, I learned about fee-based financial planning and assets under management. I discovered that managing my clients' portfolios for a fee was the secret to creating regular, recurring, predictable revenue every year. I wrote down my Master Goal of accumulating $100 million in assets under management (AUM) – the one goal that, if achieved, would nurture all of my other goals, whether they were personal, spiritual or for the family – and taped it to my bathroom mirror. I commit to it daily by repeating it like a mantra. I am well on track to reach my Master Goal within the next three years.

Once you have that goal set and can visualize it, begin to identify possible obstacles. Make a list consisting of things that could stand between you and your goals. Here is an example:

☆ Not enough clients
☆ Missing or nonexistent systems and processes
☆ Weak client service
☆ Necessity of a strong team to handle growth
☆ Effective sales presentation skills
☆ A marketing plan to generate leads

When you're creating your action steps, look for that one obstacle that is the root cause standing in the way of your success and isolate it. Once you've identified that obstacle, create a plan for overcoming it.

In my case, I needed more clients. Therefore, my action plan revolved around lead generation.

If I acquired 20 new clients per year with a minimum of $500,000 in investable assets and 20 new clients per year with a minimum of $1,000,000, I'd increase my assets under management by $30 million each year. This was doable. Or, I could acquire fifteen new clients per year, ask for two referrals per year from each client, and achieve my goal with half the work and without depleting my resources. I chose the latter. For me, the most effective way for acquiring more clients was to ask for referrals on a consistent basis. I needed a plan, a plan not that much different from the financial plans I create for my clients. I needed to take maximum action to help me reach my Master Goal.

This was my plan. I'd meet regularly with my top 25 clients and ask for referrals. It is written, "Ask and you shall receive." How profound. How simple. How easy. I identified this as my prime action: creating a referral process that would double my business each year.

If you want to double your business each year, have you considered asking for referrals in a systematic and consistent way? Referred prospects are easier to close, take less time, and cost less money. One essential ingredient in asking for referrals is to make sure your clients are happy with your service or product. Happy clients refer friends and family. If you are a business owner, talk to your happiest clients and ask them what they like the most about your service or product. Then ask them what they like the least about it. The idea is to do more of what makes your clients happy and stop doing the things they don't like.

My action plan also centered on making my clients feel special through providing more services than what my competition provided. I wanted my clients to feel proud about referring their friends. Whatever your action plan is, remember that it sometimes takes a village to help you. It's important to train and motivate your team, and compensate them accordingly, and you also need to reward yourself. Make setting and achieving goals fun for your entire team.

Keep your plan in motion and avoid the trap of over analyzing. You might get to the point where you hinder the start of your plan because you want everything to be perfect. Friedrich Engels said "An ounce of action is worth a ton of theory." Watch out for that great enemy, procrastination. Don't worry if your plan is not perfect. Look for progress. Progress is achieved by having a plan, focusing on that plan, and prioritizing your action steps. Once things are set in motion, you have the freedom to make changes as needed.

Most of us want everything, and we want it now. We want lots and lots of action since that means we're moving forward, right? Wrong. Lots of action means lots of distractions and lots of wasted time. Our time is the reservoir for all the potential that lies within us – protect it like your life depends on it, because it does. There are only so many hours in a day and so many days in a week. We cannot be all things to all people and we cannot do everything. Learn to delegate to your team so you can focus solely on those things that help you achieve your Master Goal.

If you don't know where you're going, how do you know how to get there? Define your destination. Then determine your starting point. Look at your end point and then identify a powerful financial goal that will lead you to your ultimate destination. Make this your Master Goal. Develop and implement an action plan for achieving your Master Goal.

"Yesterday is gone. Tomorrow has not yet begun.
We have only today. Let us begin."
– Mother Teresa

Focus on your Master Goal for maximum impact on your business growth; you'll achieve financial success and you'll change your life. As a wealth manager, I am devoted to helping professionals, small business owners, and key executives improve their long-term financial success by creating and implementing a plan. You may be asking yourself, "Am I on track for retirement? Will I run out of money if I retire? How can I legally pay less in taxes?" Contact me today to get help with your financial plan. Learn how you can achieve the life of your dreams through financial independence; send an email to terrie@slatenfinancial.com and type *"Step into Your Vision"* on the subject line. You'll receive a Confidential Financial Profile to get you started.

— ABOUT THE AUTHOR —

Cliff Slaten has gained substantial knowledge in the areas of business and tax planning. During the 70's, he worked as a controller and CFO for several large corporations. While holding those positions, he became interested in the virtues of American small business. Today, he is the President and CEO of Slaten Financial, a comprehensive financial planning firm committed to helping professionals, small business owners, and key executives improve their long-term financial success. www.slatenfinancial.com

CHAPTER 10

Imagine and Succeed

John Assaraf

> *"Imagination is the beginning of creation. You imagine what you desire, you will what you imagine, and at last you create what you will."*
> – George Bernard Shaw

*I*magine yourself at a beautiful beach – palm trees, white sand, the gentle roar of the waves slapping against the shoreline. Or perhaps you watch the Travel Channel and you see yourself scuba diving in Belize with schools of bright, cheerfully-colored fish swarming around you. Using the power of your imagination by visualizing on a daily basis, you can create the life you truly want to live by setting clear, precise goals and then consciously focusing your thoughts, feelings and positive actions on them daily.

To start, you need to have an absolutely clear vision of exactly what it is you want to create. You can design it in any way you want. Exercise your imagination, creativity and ingenuity – have fun! There is no limitation to your imagination. As you create a clear vision of your future, you will begin to see things you have never seen before. Miracles will happen! The key is to program your mind with visualizations, emotions and specific affirmations that support the new vision and goals you have. By regularly repeating empowering new beliefs, they will be engraved deep in your subconscious mind.

The ideal state for achieving your goals is to be motivated from deep within, to wake up excited every day, to enjoy the adventure you will have on the way to success. To motivate yourself to take action, consider how achieving your goals will make you feel. How will you act, walk, and talk when you have achieved each goal? What will you do with your new life? Come up with as many positive reasons and anchors as possible to motivate you to do your best. Don't just sit on the sidelines waiting for things to change – take charge and make your dreams come true.

Many people have seen the movie *The Secret*. If you haven't, I shared in it how I created a vision board, which is basically a board with cut-out pictures that I feel accurately depict the various goals I want to reach. This solidifies in your mind a mental image of what you want to achieve, and helps you to subliminally focus on how to achieve it. After I had moved into my current house, I opened a box of old vision boards that had been in a sealed box for over five years only to find that one of them held a picture of the house I had just bought right in the center – I had purchased my dream house without even realizing it!

There are many reasons why the vision board is so effective. Here are three of them:

1) The more specific and clear your goal is in your mind, the easier it is to achieve it.

2) If you see your goal in front of you on a regular basis, you will be more motivated to act on it.

3) When you are motivated to reach a clear, specific goal, it's easier to commit to it.

The vision board is a reminder of the power that comes from setting goals. As a matter of fact, writing down your goals is the first step towards achieving them. Why is this? When you write down your goals, your mind begins to focus on what you want, and perhaps more importantly, what you *don't* want starts to recede into the past. The more specific you are in what your goals are, the more clearly your mind can grasp what you're after. When that happens, it will get easier for you to differentiate between things that will help you reach your goals and things that will distract you from them.

Take a moment to ask yourself – What do you want to achieve in a year? Five years? Ten? Twenty? Write down your goals and make a timeline for when you want to achieve each one. Then start to make a plan. What can you do today, tomorrow, this week, next week, and so on that will move you closer to reaching those goals? It will take time and planning to figure out what it is that you really want to do, but it is definitely worth it. Remember the old expression, "Poor planning leads to poor performance." When you focus your mind on what your goals are every day and you have a plan of action for accomplishing them, you will find yourself moving toward your goals and eliminating the unnecessary things that are holding you back from reaching them.

Design your vision and write out your goals until they are perfect on paper and in your mind. Create your vision board. Plan for success, and then take action. Every time you set your goals higher, stay focused and make sure you're imprinting them on your subconscious mind. Allow them to work for you!

What if you still find yourself procrastinating, or not reaching your goals? George Naope, a great kahuna of Hawaii, says, "Take responsibility for everything that happens in your life, everything good and everything bad, as if you created it." This can be a tough concept to swallow, but the benefits are undeniable. When you take responsibility in this manner, every event in your life becomes an opportunity for feedback and improvement on the deepest of levels. Why are you dragging your feet? What excuses have you made for yourself? Pay attention to how you feel when you voice aloud what your goals are. Do they pump you up? Sometimes it can be that we are pursuing goals that we are not really in alignment with. If it turns out that they're not really something that you want deep inside, change directions and go for something that you do want.

Once you know that your goals are ones that you really want, stay focused and commit to doing the neural reconditioning work day in and day out. Make yourself reminder notes to review where you stand with the process, perhaps at the beginning of every week. Add a statement to your reprogramming routine that addresses your commitment, something along the lines of, "I am building on a solid, new, unconscious foundation to take my success even further."

So, in review: Write down what your goals are, and come up with a plan to achieve them. Focus on your goals constantly. Create your own vision board to reinforce your goals on a subconscious level. If you find yourself suffering from a lack of motivation, examine your goals to make sure they're really what you want – if they're not, find new ones. Keep yourself flexible and open to any possible means of achieving your goals, not just what you think you need to do. And finally, after you have achieved what you wanted to do, set new, higher goals for yourself, and start the process over again. If you do this, you will see the benefits of visualization in your own life, and you will reach your goals.

The real gift here is to constantly trade your life for things that are worthy of it. Don't ever ask yourself if you are worthy of your goals. . . ask if your goals are worthy of you and then act boldly to achieve those goals.

— ABOUT THE AUTHOR —

John Assaraf, a leader in the area of spiritual entrepreneurship, has built five multi-million-dollar businesses in the last twenty years. John's passions are his family, spirituality, exercise, cooking, travel, and helping entrepreneurs understand how to incorporate the psychological and strategic sides of building a successful business and life into their plans. You can learn more about John and his groundbreaking brain research and approach to earning more money and living your ideal life at www.praxisnow.com.

CHAPTER 11

True Wellness – from the Inside Out

Debra Jones

> *"What lies behind us and what lies before us are tiny matters compared to what lies within us."*
> – Ralph Waldo Emerson

"*M*ommie. . . why are you crying, Mommie?" My little girl looked at me with her big, innocent eyes; I could see the pain in her heart as she saw me lying on the bathroom floor. She didn't understand what was going on, but she sensed something was really wrong. This was the wake-up call I needed. For 15 years I had been playing the "happy wife," and I had become pretty darn good at it—nobody would have known it was all a façade. I was so good, I believed it myself – until the emotional pain became so intense I would hit myself physically in an effort to release my self-hatred. I figured that if I would make enough to get us out of debt, things would get better. But my efforts only took us further into debt. I was tired of my life—I just wanted to be well.

What is holding you back from achieving your goals? Can it be that under the surface there is more going on? When you are not authentic, it is hard to achieve your goals—a strong undercurrent of limiting beliefs and negative self-talk can keep you down and prevent you from living up to the greatness you have inside.

Back then, I didn't have the awareness to understand that my self-sabotaging environment had a major stranglehold on me. I didn't love myself enough to notice. It wasn't until I saw how my 18-month-old daughter was being affected that something inside me shifted. The pain of changing had become less than the pain of staying the same.

When you decide in your heart it's time to change, take courageous action from a place of faith and love; God will direct your steps. When I picked up a Pilates book, it didn't seem like a big deal at the time. Looking back, that book became the catalyst that changed my life forever.

There is a powerful connection between bodies and mind that we in Western Society tend to neglect. I was simply a new mom who needed exercise to lose weight and release anxiety. As I began to move my body with mindful control, I experienced the strengthening power of Pilates working from the deepest muscles at the body's center, with conscious control. Focusing on my body and breath anchored me in the present moment, and more than my body began to transform. When you train your body from the inside out, not only do you tone it, you find the connection to your true self and your external environment. As your awareness begins to expand, like a light shining brighter into the fog around you, you'll find clarity on the changes you need to make.

In order to be true to yourself, your beliefs need to reflect your values and be congruent with your divine purpose. A toxic environment, a self-sabotaging lifestyle and a destructive inner voice hold you back from reaching your goals, as you are using all your energy to fight the battle within. Most of us have beliefs that don't serve us well. That is why it is important to have support and guidance to strengthen and recreate your core beliefs. Body and soul are connected; by taking a holistic approach, you will know your true self—whole, centered, and self-aware—and experience real well-being.

Stepping into your greatness takes courage; it can be a tough battle to break free from your old habits, patterns, beliefs and lifestyle. It is hard, if not impossible, to journey this path alone. Aligning yourself with people who value health, wholeness and abundance, you will build a team that believes in you before you believe in yourself. Their support can empower you to emerge triumphantly.

What is it you want to achieve? Are you willing to do whatever it takes to get it? Do you know what you "should" be doing but keep allowing life to get in the way? Are you playing small? Do not settle. You can enjoy greater health and abundance. What is holding you back from creating the life you desire and experiencing authentic happiness?

Live in wholeness and well-being

In order to live in wholeness and well-being, you need to:

☆ Acknowledge your greatness. Most people are oblivious to their greatness and do not realize the secret desire they hold in their heart to change and become extraordinary; their world is glowing behind the dark and heavy obstacles that they have learned to gravitate around. When a glimpse of this light reveals itself, capture the moment—reach out, take action before the calluses close the gap and deflect the rays of your deepest desires.

☆ Give yourself permission to live and be happy; live with an open heart and allow wonderful things to flow into your life.

☆ Be authentic. You are an original; reveal your true self, find your voice, honor your feelings and the intrinsic urge to be healthy and happy. Living authentically is essential to true peace within.

☆ Let go of your story. Your story doesn't define you or who you are. This awakening can enable you to remove any sticky residue from an old banner marked "damaged goods—no declared value." Replace negative self-talk with affirmations and positive feelings.

☆ Grow in awareness. Mindful movement taught me how to anchor in the present moment—life itself—which I now seize. Once you embark on this journey, there is no turning back: compromise, conformity and mediocrity are no longer tolerated.

☆ Set and accomplish goals that are in alignment with your values, principles and purpose. A supportive environment is essential for you to realize your dreams and desires. If you are in a situation that you need to change or remove yourself from in order for you to achieve your purpose, surround yourself with a team of like-minded people. Choose your doctors, therapists, advisors, mentors and coaches, friends and partners wisely because the people closest to you will dramatically affect all areas of your life.

☆ Experience real success. Many people appear to be successful, but their health or relationships greatly lag behind their financial gain, leaving them hopeless, because they do not have the necessary mental and physical health or companionship to enjoy their rewards.

☆ Celebrate! There is never a small accomplishment—each one is worth celebrating! They give us energy to fuel our power to overcome the next challenge.

Physical fitness is the first requisite of happiness.
- Joseph Pilates

Every morning I wake up happy. Thanks to the people around me, I dropped from a size 12-14 to a 6-8 effortlessly, as a result of removing the stranglehold of a long-standing, self-sabotaging lifestyle; I am debt free and well on my way to achieving greater financial goals. Committing to a life-long study of Pilates, it was a natural extension to become a certified instructor and a professional wellness coach.

As a mother of a wonderful daughter, animal lover, friend to many, entrepreneur, business owner and now author, I know how important your health is in order to have the energy to live well. My team does not tolerate me playing small. I am ultimately responsible for my choices and how I react to life, which provides me true happiness. My daughter will never again find me weak from self-destructive behaviors. I am a mindful parent and an autonomous woman who operates in her power, out of love for self. I never had imagined this was possible – or even a choice. Now I am able to set and accomplish goals that are in alignment with my values and purpose, which gives me great inner peace—and true wholeness.

You, too, can choose to overcome adversity, change your limiting beliefs and live a passionate, extraordinary life! You are creative, resourceful and whole. You have the power within you to achieve your greatest dreams and desires.

When you would like me to be a part of your team to help you improve an area of wellness—whether fitness, nutrition, weight, stress, health, or life challenges that impact your wellness—contact me to schedule your 40-minute complimentary coaching session. I would be honored to partner with you. You'll find more information about this offer at the special website I've created for readers of this book at http://berealbewell.com/goals.html. Your compass and your guide – that is all within you; however, I will coach you as you chart your new course, and empower you to achieve your set goals as you experiment with a new way of living in health, wholeness and well-being.

— ABOUT THE AUTHOR —

Debra Jones, owner of BodyMindBusiness LLC, is internationally recognized for transforming lives through an intuitive and holistic approach to wellness. She is a graduate of one of the most innovative and comprehensive Health Coach Training programs available. She is classically trained in Pilates and she is comprehensively certified through Peak Pilates. Debra empowers her clients to see the truth that is already inside of them so they may gain conscious control of their lives in order to express their true self and find authentic happiness, the core of real wellness. Link: http://berealbewell.com/goals.html. Deb@BodyMindBusiness.com

CHAPTER 12

Smell the Roses

Andrea Harlin

> *"When faced with a mountain, I will not quit! I will keep striving until I climb over, find a pass through, tunnel underneath or simply stay and turn the mountain into a gold mine, with God's help."*
> – Dr. Robert Schuller

*M*y life was perfect. My family was doing well—our son had graduated from high school and was in college. I had been his personal driver – because he didn't drive – at first. From the day he was born he had been my top priority, and I was proud to see him develop into such a wonderful young man. The summer before, my husband and I had been to Hawaii to celebrate our anniversary. We had gone through our difficulties in the past, but at that point, everything was great. I was active in our church and in our community. Katrina had just hit New Orleans and I was glad I could help my relatives who were affected by the hurricane. Life was good and the future looked bright.

My career path had been very fulfilling. I had worked with children that had been in foster care for a long time. After that, I worked for a church. I helped to set up a community clinic and had run my own consultancy.

My varied experiences lead me to a job working in five different school district programs, which meant that every week, I visited 12 facilities. I enjoyed working in every aspect of the family support programs. It was exciting to be in different places. But I always needed a little something to shoot for, so I decided to get my real estate license to have some fun and get another career going, instead of becoming bored. I enjoyed the variety and challenges of my life. Little did I know that my whole life was about to change drastically…

Sometimes we can get so caught up in achieving our goals, we are so focused on where we want to be, that we forget to smell the roses; we stomp through the beautiful rose beds like an elephant, without even noticing them.

January 23rd: I had felt ill over the weekend, as I was cramming for the real estate exam. I went to work on Monday anyway, but I started to feel worse, and was coughing up thick mucus. On Tuesday, I went to see the doctor; she said I had bronchitis and gave me antibiotics. A week later she gave me more antibiotics, as I wasn't getting better. The asthma was so bad I could hardly breathe, so she gave me even more antibiotics. In addition, the physician assistant gave me steroids, which made my brain swell. I had a bad cough and couldn't even walk anymore… I was getting sicker and sicker.

I stopped taking the steroids and decided to stay home for a few days. I wanted to get back to work, because I knew it was hard to find subs, but I didn't have a voice, I could hardly breathe and I had terrible headaches. Despite the 12 medications I was taking, the doctor couldn't get anything under control. This lasted for two years. Every time I went back to work, I would get sicker. The school district was willing to work with me. My husband would drive me to work and pick me up, but it didn't work; the medications had messed up my immune system.

Eventually, I discovered that I had whooping cough. It is very rare, but occurs more in certain communities, according to a doctor I met who had traveled a lot. Sadly enough, the neurologist told me that there was nothing that could be done to restore the damage to my body caused by the medications I had taken. It has been a journey, and it still is. I focus on what I can do instead of what I can't do anymore.

It has been a very difficult time, yet in the pain, there are valuable lessons to learn:

☆ Take time to smell the roses

It's great to set goals, make a plan and work hard to achieve them, but always remember to stop and smell the roses. When you are moving at a very high pace, you may miss out on all the beautiful things that surround you every day. With a speed of 99 miles per minute, it's pretty much impossible to even see the roses. Appreciate the small things in life—don't take them for granted just because you have a big vision for your life.

☆ Count your blessings

No matter how challenging life may get, you still have reasons to be grateful. Despite the fact that I can't do what I used to, I am still here. Even though I am very weak, I am alive. My son has given me a lot of strength. My husband and my parents have really been there for me and they are happy that I'm still here. Count your blessings.

☆ Adjust your goals

Sometimes you have to accept that what you had in mind is no longer possible, and you may have to readjust your goals. For me, driving myself to physical therapy was a goal I was proud to have achieved. No matter what it takes, don't give up; even if you have to break your goals down into smaller chunks, keep moving forward to reach your goals.

☆ *Find strength in forgiveness*

You don't want other people defining you or your reality. Decide to forgive those who may have hurt you in the past. This will allow you to let go and move on with your own life. It wasn't easy to forgive my doctor. Not only had she caused significant damage to my body by prescribing so many wrong medications, she had also told me I was imagining my illness because she couldn't find the problem.

☆ *Be open to change*

Don't be afraid to make major life changes, spiritually, mentally or physically, when you are faced with major life challenges. Maybe you can't work eight hours a day for a boss. Even if you can only work for an hour, you are still in control of your life. There are always options.

☆ *Hold on to God*

Regardless of what happens, when God is with you, there is nothing you can't overcome. No matter how difficult your life may be, you need your relationship with God.

> *"For all things I have the strength by virtue*
> *of him who imparts power to me."*
> – Philippians 4:13

I now help people start their own businesses and provide the tools and training to be successful. My passion is to teach entrepreneurs how to set and achieve their goals, reduce stress, improve their relationships and earn more money! Discover the 5 Best Steps to Profit from *Your* Business. Get your FREE 7-Day Email Course at www.aesc21entrepreneur.com.

— ABOUT THE AUTHOR —

Andrea Harlin is a graduate of Cal State University Dominguez Hills. She has more than 25 years of experience as a business counselor and educator. As a vocational counselor, she guided high school students and adults to their right career paths, as well as held them accountable for achieving their goals. She also worked with them to reduce stress. Andrea has been featured on radio programs and has received various awards for community services. She is the author of *How to Have Fun with Home Work*. Call her to schedule a free consultation at 1-800-527-4184 or email her at laaes8@gmail.com.

Like An Eagle

When life knocks you to the ground
Disappointments draining your energy
Tap into the source of abundance
Filling your soul with refreshing chi

When people hurt your feelings
Emotional wounds making you weak
Spread your wings to catch the wind
Feeling the power provided for the meek

When the pain permeates every cell in your being
And the grief is too hard to bear
Open your heart in prayer
Knowing that God is there

When your world crumbles under your feet
Your dreams coming to naught
Give thanks for all you still have
Experiencing the peace of God that excels all thought

When you are desperate and in despair
Wondering if you'll ever reach your goal
Become like an eagle
Hoping in Jehovah with all your soul

Like an eagle you will …
Fly at incredible heights
Soar beyond your wildest imagination
Mount up with dynamic energy
Live a fulfilling life

– Shamayah

Based on Isaiah 40:29-31, Philippians 4:7,13 and Proverbs 3:34

CHAPTER 13

Everything is Possible

Andrew Aaron

"With men this is impossible,
but with God all things are possible."
— Matthew 19:26

The New Orleans of 1932 was not the same bustling and colorful tourist city that it is today. The city I grew up in was separated into two different societies: that of whites and blacks. Sure, I could go play at the local park with my friends, but I couldn't drink water from the same fountains as the white people, no matter how thirsty I was. Like many other people, I would ride the city bus downtown. My ticket was paid for, just like everyone else's, but even though there were plenty of empty seats to choose from, because of our skin color, blacks had to sit as far to the back of the vehicle as possible – each and every time. Clothing stores would happily take our money, but we weren't allowed to try them on in the store. It was humiliating; we were treated as second-class individuals in our own country, the United States of America. Sadly, many blacks, after being subjected to this false and hurtful mindset for far too long, actually began believing (whether consciously or sub-consciously) that they deserved nothing better.

You may have experienced similar situations in your life, when those around you tried to put you down. No matter what you have been through personally, you have inside of you what it takes to build a better life for yourself and your family. Walk with me down my path of adversity and triumph and discover how you, too, can rise above life's negative circumstances and achieve your own personal dreams, desires and ambitions.

It Starts on the Inside

Throughout my childhood, my mother and grandmother's words, "Andrew, you are special! You are a smart boy and you can do anything!" resonated loudly with me. While I may not have realized it consciously as a young child, that statement filled me with aspiration and self-worth. I believed I could do anything, so I never let anyone or anything stand in my way! Despite my everyday surroundings, I was so incredibly blessed to have the love and encouragement of wonderful parents and grandparents who believed in me in ALL aspects of my life. This, combined with the daily examples of their own hard work and confidence, built up and strengthened my own belief in myself. It was then that I knew that I could actually achieve my dreams of providing a good life for myself and my family and that I would NEVER be defined by the color of my skin.

Even if you didn't have people around you who encouraged you when you were young, you can decide today what you want to believe about yourself. When someone tells you that you can't do something, you have to tell yourself, "If they can do it, I can do it!" As an army man, I was passed over for a promotion by a psychologist who believed I would not excel because of my parents' divorce, despite my high test scores. I proved him wrong, earning many commendations and medals, and eventually being promoted to Sergeant in the field.

Resilience is Key

As a child, I learned the value of hard work and determination. I was very motivated by watching my mother and uncle run their grocery store. My uncle was one of the first black grocers in New Orleans, Louisiana, and he had a job with the city of New Orleans, as well. My father and grandfather worked as railroad brakemen, a rare thing for black Americans at the time, and that inspired me. I wanted to be educated, because I realized, "If you learn more, you earn more!" In my mind, the only way to change my destiny was through education and real estate ownership.

At that time, property ownership by blacks was almost unheard of, yet I watched my parents and grandparents work multiple jobs to achieve that goal. Thanks to their hard work and diligent saving, they could buy a house where we lived together. The harsh reality was that no matter how hard they worked to achieve their goals, life wasn't fair in those days. One day, the state seized my grandparents' property—the home where we would come together as a family, the home that all of us were so proud of and that they had made so many sacrifices for, was taken. It was a very sad and painful experience, but despite the setback, my family didn't give up on their dream to create a better future for the generations to come.

You have to be willing to learn, work hard, and realize that despite your hard work, you will face setbacks and disappointments in life. When that happens, you can't give up. You can't give in whether you fell off or someone threw you off, you have to be resilient and get back on your horse.

Focus Daily on Your Goal

A key in attaining your aims is to set your goals and objectives and work them daily. Stay focused on your goals by speaking or writing them down. Tell yourself, "This is what I'm going to do!" and share it with others. Reaffirm your goals every day to stay focused and accomplish what you want in your life. Once you have set your mind on something, it's a matter of time, dedicated effort and resilience.

When I enlisted in the Army on March 8, 1948, at 16, I was assigned to the Buffalo Soldiers – the first black professional soldiers. I thought joining the army would be different than my life back home, but the army was even worse. My unit was segregated. It was frightening, because the commanders often sent the black units into battles because it was more dangerous. We received less support from the command in many battles. When our trucks broke down, we had to fix them ourselves to save time. I wanted desperately to become an officer. I studied hard and scored well on the tests, but was still passed over. I constantly told myself that I could do it. It was a long, hard road, but I reached my goal after receiving my sixth battlefield star. I later became a Captain, having risen through the ranks.

Cherish the People You Love

Tap into the goodness in your life to see you through the rough spots. Take time to spend with your family and friends. If you get too focused on achieving your goal and are too busy for the ones you love, you miss out on true success. Even when I had multiple jobs and went to college, I would always take time off for road trips, or even just to spend Sundays with my children. Go on vacation with your family and realize how precious the time is that you get to spend with them. Let your family and friends be your guides and motivate you on your path to success!

Today, I am almost 80 years old. I'm blessed with three wonderful daughters, three beautiful grandsons, and two lovely great-grand-daughters. The cornerstones of my success are rooted in education, perseverance, family and a strong belief in God. No matter how difficult your challenges may be, remember that there is someone greater to back you up.

Nowadays, I refuse to sit at the back of the bus. I want to be treated with respect and dignity. I enjoy the nice things in life, because I deserve them—and so do you! My skin has never defined me. I am defined by my accomplishments. The only barrier to your success is you. With inspiration, drive and motivation, you too can change your circumstances and create the life you desire.

My goal now is to share my history, and that of the Buffalo Soldiers, through a museum established to help people become aware of other cultures and enjoy what they have shared, as well as know how they have worked in the United States and throughout the world. It will be a community-based cultural center where youth and their families can learn about their heritage, train for new careers and participate in parent education, anger management, and other health-related and community services. This book will be used as a launching pad to raise funds for the cultural center. Go to www.buffalosoldiersonlinemuseum.com to join our community and purchase Buffalo Soldier commemorative coins in a limited edition set or call 800-670-9049.

— ABOUT THE AUTHOR —

 Andrew Aaron, Jr. is a decorated, retired Army Major. He was a member of the Buffalo Soldiers. Inspired by his love, God and his family, he opened doors of opportunity. Mr. Aaron has dedicated himself to the development of a Buffalo Soldier Museum and Cultural Center in the Los Angeles area. He hopes that this effort will inspire others from all backgrounds to achieve their goals, even in the face of adversity. www.buffalosoldiersonlinemuseum.com. Email: aabos@aabos.com

The Magic of Goal Setting

Judy O'Higgins

> *"One of the amazing things we have been given as humans is the unquenchable desire to have dreams of a better life, and the ability to establish goals to live out those dreams."*
> – Jim Rohn

It was January, 2005. I was having a cup of coffee and feeling depressed, as I had every day for the past three months. I had joined a network marketing company eight years earlier, with the hope of building my own retirement plan. My dream had crashed and burned along with that company, and I was thinking, I will never be able to retire. Like many Baby Boomers, I had not saved enough for my retirement, and I was also experiencing burnout from my counseling career. I couldn't see any other options than to just keep doing what I had been for 25 years—uplift people who needed counseling for life issues. I needed a change, but financially, I could not stop working. I prayed for a solution.

The phone rang that rainy afternoon. "Let it go to voice mail," I thought. I didn't want to take the call until I saw the number on my caller

ID. It was Jordan Adler! He had been my trainer and inspiration in that network marketing company! I had always respected and looked up to Jordan for his incredible training and his amazing success. "Why would he be calling me now?" I wondered aloud. I picked up the phone.

We talked about old times. Then, he started to excitedly share information about a small, young company with a unique product—a personal relationship-building system with greeting cards that used technology to semi-automate the process. My spirit felt alive for the first time in months. The good news: here was another way to uplift people without having to listen to their life problems! The bad news: I had no background in sales, and was pretty shy when outside the comfort zone of my counseling office. I felt myself standing on the edge of a cliff—should I stay in my safe comfort zone and work for more years at the only thing I knew, or take a risk and jump off the cliff into a new and unknown world that had the potential to set me financially free, but held no guarantees? I decided in that moment to let go of my fear and take the leap!

When you take a leap of faith, you get outside your comfort zone. You often don't have the skills and experience to succeed in this new arena and you'll have to learn, practice and execute new behaviors.

Let me share with you the strategies that helped me to become one of the top 1% money earners in my company, and achieve my goal of retiring as a counselor.

☆ Set a Big Goal

Don't be afraid to dream big. What is your heart's desire? Don't shrink your dream to match your current circumstances. You have to be passionate about your goal, so it will inspire you to move consistently forward despite all challenges.

☆ *Mentors are Key*

Do not try to figure everything out yourself. When you want to start a new business and don't know anything about the process of sales, systems and goal setting, find somebody who can help you. Jordan Adler continued to be a great mentor for me, and so was Eric Lofholm. Remain coachable and open to continued personal growth to be successful in the long run. It is a never-ending process.

☆ *The Power of Planning & Written Goals*

One of the best concepts Eric taught me was the power of written goals. Write your business plan and think of what outcomes you want for your business. Break that plan down into monthly goals, then weekly goals, and finally list the six most important things to achieve every day. By applying this goal-setting process, my business grew faster and more robustly!

☆ *Take Action Every Day*

Create and write down short-term goals toward your big dream goal, and take clear action steps every week toward your dream. Do something every day to move your business forward. Don't let fear of learning new skills kill your dream. Set small step-by-step goals for yourself to overcome your fear and take action daily until it is no longer difficult.

This is an example of the weekly goals I set for myself, and executed over and over, until it became easy:

1) Attend one to three networking events per week.
2) Meet and connect with a minimum of two new people at these events.
3) Practice a script of what to say to create interest.
4) Follow up with a card and a phone call.
5) Introduce prospective customers to our card and gift service through a demonstration and free sample, again using a script and following a sequence of actions.

6) Continue to follow up and build a relationship if they are not ready to purchase our product or join our business at the time of the demonstration.

7) For those who buy our card and gift program, provide them custom training on how to use it for their particular industry.

When you start to see the results of your actions, like I did, it will give you the confidence you need to keep moving forward. My first goal was to have 1,000 people on my team. Within two years, I achieved this goal and my dream of retiring had come true, with only part-time effort. What if I had chosen to stay "safe" and not jump off that cliff? I would have never achieved the dream that had seemed so out of reach just two years earlier.

When you have achieved your initial goals, start to dream bigger dreams and play a bigger game. As you expand your vision, your life could begin a new chapter, once again challenging your comfort zone and causing you to set new and bigger goals. Because of the economic downturn and resulting job losses, retirement nest eggs that have vanished or shrunk, and dreams that have been forgotten or put on hold, I made a new goal in 2009 to write a book showing other women how to achieve financial freedom through starting a network marketing business. In the fall of 2010, I completed this goal along with two exceptional women co-authors, Kristi Lee and Karen Palmer, and our book, *License to Dream-Every Woman's Guide to Financial Freedom through Network Marketing*, has become a reality!

Goal setting was again instrumental in this project. In the fall of 2009, the three of us met and set an intention to write this book and have it published within a year. We had a common goal of inspiring millions of women to get their dreams back through network marketing – and because so many had been negatively affected by the economy, there was no time to waste. The process was challenging since all three of us were running our home businesses and had family or other responsibilities in our lives, and not much "free time" — but we did it! We were able to finish our book and get it published in the fall of 2010, even with all of our other life challenges.

How? By writing clear goals specifying who would be responsible for what, holding ourselves and each other accountable, setting completion deadlines, and supporting each other through the process. That is why we devoted an entire chapter of our book to goal setting! In 2011, we went on to complete a CD set and workbook based on the principles in our book, and even put on our first two-day success seminar for women in network marketing!

My world is much bigger and more exciting today than it was seven years ago when I began my journey as a network marketing entrepreneur! Many thanks to Eric Lofholm for teaching me the amazing power of goal setting. I hope I have inspired you to do the same to realize your dreams. Today, I am the leader of a team of over 5,000 distributors and am "paying it forward" by teaching them leadership skills and the power of written goals. All this from someone who knew zero about entrepreneurship, but had a dream to create my retirement and the good sense to learn from my mentors, set goals and take daily action.

Today, it is my passion to inspire you to believe that you can reach your dreams. I also love to coach women to greater success in network marketing. You can make your dreams come true, but you can't do it on your own. Email me at judy@networkmarketingdreamteam.com to receive a free 20-minute coaching session to help you succeed.

— ABOUT THE AUTHOR —

Judy O'Higgins is an entrepreneur who achieved her goal of creating her own retirement with passive income from her network marketing company, SendOutCards. Judy has built a team with over 5,000 people and is ranked in the top 1% of her company. She has co-authored a book and audio series teaching women of all ages how to be successful in network marketing and achieve their dreams. *License to Dream-Every Woman's Guide to Financial Freedom through Network Marketing* is available, along with the CD set and workbook, at www.networkmarketingdreamteam.com.

CHAPTER 15

Achieve Your Goals,
Faster, Easier, Simpler

Aristotle Karas

*"Don't be afraid of losing, be afraid of playing
a game and not learning something."*
– Dan Heisman

There I was, after a long flight, in Egypt. I was excited to experience the culture and explore the country. I had been looking forward to this trip for nearly a year! I had all the things I wanted to see and do planned. I picked up my bags from the conveyor belt when suddenly, total panic struck! I had made great plans, but in my excitement, I thought I had forgotten to look up where the University of Cairo was or make arrangements for my first night. Then I remembered the email from six months earlier that said the University would have somebody pick me up. The color returned in my face. Was there a car already waiting for me?

I walked outside—there were many signs with all kind of names, but none that read "Aristotle." I was in the desert, yet I was not sweating from the heat alone. After a while most people were picked up, but I was still there, miles away from home, all by myself. In exhaustion, I turned around and saw a man holding a sign I had not seen before: AUC. Suddenly it dawned on me—of course! I had been so blinded by what I thought the sign was supposed to say that I had not seen what was right there in front of me all that time: AUC—American University of Cairo. I had found my driver.

☆ Expect the unexpected

That day I learned a valuable lesson—the road to your goal could look completely different than you expected. Sometimes, you have such a strong idea of what something should look like that it narrows your vision and you miss the opportunity right in front of you. Often, if you remain open and flexible, a path of lesser resistance surfaces. I can only imagine the ensuing nightmare if I had not seen the sign "AUC" and had to make my own way to the university. Maybe I would still be lost in Cairo today…

Take a step back. What opportunities are right in front of you? Could there be another way to achieve your goals? Sometimes the best road is right in front of you, as in my case. When you shift the way you look at the world, new doors open. Remain alert for the little signs while staying focused on the larger end result. The universe will show you how to get there. Sometimes, what seems like a detour or a setback is actually a step in the right direction.

One of my goals was to build a successful auction company. I didn't plan to go into software, but when the opportunity presented itself to develop a software auction company, I realized it could be the mechanism to achieve my main goal—build a successful company to provide for my family. The road to my goal was different from what I expected it to be, yet the destination was the same.

☆ Failing is ok

Failure is part of the formula for success. It is ok to fail and not meet your goal. Often, our greatest lessons come from our biggest failures. If you fall nine times, just get up and make it the 10th time. When I was playing chess with my friend, Greg, I realized that I had become a good player because I had learned from the many times I lost.

You are not limited by your own mistakes; you can also learn from those of others. How do you achieve your goal if you have never done something and have yet to acquire the skills? You learn from others—hire someone, find mentors, seek qualified advice. A mentor can help you see things from a different angle. When you are playing chess, it is harder to see what is happening because you are emotionally involved and attached to the outcome. A friend may step into the room, look over the board, and have a completely different view. He or she can give you advice on different moves to make, ones you didn't see, because you saw the board only from your perspective. That is why it is important to listen to feedback if you want to become successful.

In the real estate auction industry, you don't get paid if you don't close the deal. That could mean eight to nine weeks of unpaid labor. Sometimes things may not work out the way you wanted, but there can still be value in what you learned. Prepare better for the next time and learn from your failures and mistakes. Experience gives you foresight.

I had the opportunity to sell a $14.6 million property in Hawaii, but lacked the experience to do it; I had never sold a home in Hawaii nor a decamillion dollar property. So I called Marty, the most experienced auctioneer in the country I knew, to help me. Big lesson: you need experience to achieve your goals, so use your own or borrow someone else's.

☆ A king cannot win a battle by himself

In chess, as in business, there are different pieces to the game: the board, pawns, bishops, knights, castles, queens, and kings. Which one are you? You can't wear all the hats. The king needs to understand how to move the other pieces. It's helpful to know the different roles, but it's not needed to play them all. Hire people with the skill sets that are not your strongest talents. Are you the one on the road day after day? Do you spend most of your time supporting someone else's efforts? I came to realize that I don't have to be the best bid caller to run a successful auction company. However, my experience as an auctioneer taught me to organize successful events.

I would rather be the king who watches and commands. If I am up there selling with the microphone, I have to stay in that role and I can't command what is happening at the event. Even though you have valuable experience, you can't be the King when you are playing different, subordinate roles.

Sometimes, you have to accept that you are not a king. If your company runs better when you, "the boss," are not around, it is time to hire a CEO. You can still own the company; just know your best position. You can pay yourself as a knight and company owner.

It is critical to understand that each piece on the board has its role and purpose. You can't win with only a king. A king cannot fight all the battles all the time by him- or herself. Know when one of your own pieces is in the way of success; don't be afraid to remove it.

As the king, you need to develop good leadership skills. The best way to lead is to learn how to follow. Enroll in leadership and self-development seminars. Empower the people working for you by entrusting them with responsibilities. Being a strong leader is powerful. Whether it is an employee, a contractor or a vendor, they will raise their level or step out of the way if they know they can't meet your expectations.

In order to be successful you have to evaluate yourself:
- Do I have the skill sets to achieve my goal?
- Do I need to develop better skills, hire those who compensate for my weaknesses or find a partner?
- What is my role in my company? Is that the right role for me?
- Which roles am I missing? Which roles need improvement?

Looking at yourself entails facing your own incompetencies and deficiencies; a faulty premise leads to flawed planning. A great team sheds light on the truth and complements your strengths. Accept the fact that you will make mistakes. Accept the truth that your company will at times flounder. Remain focused on your goals despite the circumstances. In life, you win some, you lose some – but as in any game, you don't stand a chance of winning unless you *keep playing.*

My mission is to put more profit into the non-profit industry. Sometimes, a third party overview is needed to jolt an organization to profitability. If you are involved in or support a non-profit organization that needs more money to achieve its goals of helping people—whether it is supporting the latest disaster relief program, fighting cancer, helping teenage moms stay in school, or something as simple as raising money for your kids' school—contact us today; we can make a difference! We empower non-profit organizations by teaching them how to run successful fundraising events and be highly profitable. Go to www.secretsoffundraising.com/bookspecial to get your FREE e-book *"10 Secrets of Successful Fundraising."*

"Fundraising made Faster, Easier, Simpler."

— ABOUT THE AUTHOR —

Aristotle Karas is a speaker and auctioneer who has shared the stage with Harrison Ford, Morgan Freeman, Les Brown and Loral Langemeier, to name a few. Aristotle has consulted with non-profits of all sizes, pioneering one of the first mobile auction apps and event management systems. He has been featured in several publications, including the NAA's Auctioneer Magazine and The Wall Street Journal. His solution for increasing fundraising revenues is changing the non-profit industry by storm. www.SecretsofFundraising.com

CHAPTER 16

Your Beliefs become Your Reality

Kenneth Teninty

"A man without a goal is like a ship without a rudder."
– Thomas Carlyle

$\mathcal{W}$ hatever you desire in your life will happen, as long as you believe it and take the right actions towards achieving it. Are you living the life you want? Do you know where you would like to be, what you would like to be, what you would like to have, what would you like to do, in the next six months? What about this time next year, five years or even 10 years from now? If not, it's time to set some personal goals!

Goals are vital to your success. What you focus on, you will get. How can you hit a goal if you do not have one? You must have and commit to your own goals. A goal without a commitment is just an idea. It is never too late to set goals. Goals are a great way to keep you focused, reduce stress and be creative at a high level.

Goal setting is a powerful way of motivating yourself. It is essential to managing your time well, because it gives you a direction and purpose to work toward. When you know where you want to go, you can manage your priorities, time, and resources to get there. The only thing standing between you and your goals is your decision to make it happen.

Napoleon Hill said, *"Whatever the mind of man can conceive and bring itself to believe, it can achieve."* Do you believe this? One individual did. A young man born in Appleton, Wisconsin, grew up wanting to be a professional football player. He was told he was too small to play professionally. He was 5 foot 9 inches tall, weighed 212 pounds and had played college football at Notre Dame. Upon graduation in 1968, he was drafted in the 16th round by the NFL. He was also drafted by the US Army a few months later and sent to Vietnam. In 1969, he was wounded and told he wouldn't walk again. In 1970, he was placed on the injured reserve list for the football team that had drafted him in 1968. He was transferred to the Taxi Squad in 1971, and by 1972, was on the active roster. In 1974, he earned a spot in the starting backfield for the Pittsburgh Steelers. His name is Rocky Bleier, now a four-time Super Bowl Champion.

A study conducted at Yale University placed goal setters firmly in the successful category when compared to non-goal setters. The 3 percent of participants who had written their goals with a plan and took consistent action were happier, more confident and better adjusted. They also earned more money over a 20-year period than the remaining 97 percent of participants.

As a child, I traveled a lot. You could say we moved with the seasons— that is, potato season, orange season, apple season, string bean season… well, I think you get the point. I attended at least two schools a year up to the time I graduated from high school. The one thing I did know was that for things to change in my life, I had to change. I'm not special or better than anyone else. However, I did have some big dreams to realize, and I had the belief that I could accomplish whatever I wanted. You see, I was always told you can do whatever you put your mind to. All you had to do is make a decision, believe it and go for it. Without really knowing what I was doing, I would decide on something, commit to completing it and persist until I achieved the result I was looking for.

The turning point in my life was when I discovered that goal setting is a process that can help you achieve your goals faster if you follow all the required steps. Here are just a few of the goals I have achieved:

– I like to travel: I have been to Germany, France, Belgium, Luxemburg, the Netherlands, Austria, East Germany (at the time, and before my 35th birthday), the eastern Caribbean islands, Hawaii, and I'm still going.

– I wanted to get my college degree. I received my BA degree from Columbia College, MO, and my Master's from Drexel University, PA. While attending college, I was able to cut my study time in half by learning proper study skills. (By the way, I am the first and only one in my family to obtain a college education.)

– In October 2010, I wrote three goals down: change career, write a book and pay off a quarter of my debt. Results: In November, I changed careers; in December, I paid a third of my debt off; in February, 2012, my first book was published.

> *"You can get everything you want faster*
> *than you ever thought possible."*
> – Brian Tracy

You truly can receive everything you want faster than you ever thought possible. It happened for me and it can happen for you.

The results are amazing when you follow these steps:

☆ *Write*

The first step is to write your goals down, because this will set everything in motion. Writing your goals will help you achieve them faster than you can possibly imagine. The more focused you are on your goals, the more likely you are to accomplish them. It is also extremely important to review your goals several times during the day.

☆ Believe

Without believing you can achieve your goals, it will not happen. What you think about most of the time you will achieve. Stay positive. The most common reason for failing to meet your goals is often a mental block or limiting belief.

☆ Visualize

Be clear about what you want. Write your goals down. Visualize already achieving them, in the present. See them, feel them, smell them, touch them, taste them. Think how your life will be once you have what you want.

> *"The more you visualize yourself having achieved*
> *your goals, the more your brain decides that this is the*
> *real you and the more it works to promote the*
> *behavior that drives this to be true."*
> – Kelly Traver, MD

☆ Commit

Be committed to achieving your goals. Do something every day to accomplish them. If you need to change a goal, do not consider it a failure. Consider it a victory that you had the insight to realize something had to be changed. Most of all, be happy and have fun.

Are you ready to STOP making excuses and START making progress? Are you ready to start living your life with purpose, determination and tenacity? Then use this simple four-step process of visualizing, believing, writing them down and committing to doing something every day towards your goals. This will change your life and your future. Remember: the only thing standing between you and your goals is your decision to make it happen. I urge you to invest the time.

It's not too late. You have NO EXCUSES. Take action today, and create the life you want to live.

> *"To accomplish great things, we must not only act but also dream, not only plan but also believe."*
> – Anatole France

— ABOUT THE AUTHOR —

 Ken Teninty is a speaker, author, trainer and consultant, providing motivational and educational seminars to educational institutions and to a variety of organizations. Ken has a Bachelor of Arts degree in Psychology from Columbia College and a Master of Science degree in Science of Instruction from Drexel University. His passion is to inspire people to visualize, plan and achieve their goals in life. Ken is also available to share his knowledge of Personal Development, Time Management, How to Read a Book, How to Take a Test, How to Take Notes, and more. You may contact Ken at 210-744-9337 or msgken@hotmail.com.

CHAPTER 17

Is Your House Built with Straw, Wood or Brick?

Pauline Bourne

> *"A clear vision, backed by definite plans, gives you a tremendous feeling of confidence and personal power."*
> – Brian Tracy

*R*emember the tale of *The Three Little Pigs*? Imagine yourself being one of the little pigs setting out into the world to build your house. Of course you want to be the little pig who builds its house with bricks, the sturdiest and most secure of the materials available. You build a strong foundation and a reliable framework. Next, you start to build rooms, each serving a specific purpose based on your exact needs. In no time, through great planning and diligent work, your house is complete and ready for you to move in. Over time, you make a few updates, adjustments and repairs to maintain the value of your house, as well as to keep everything functioning properly. Through careful planning, you discover that you are one smart little pig: safe and sound out of reach of the Big Bad Wolf.

Your dreams are your destinations, your aspirations and the starting point of your road to financial independence. They are essential for the design of your financial house. Once you know your dreams, they have to be turned into powerful goals to build a solid foundation. After 30 years in the life insurance industry, I have seen the difference in the quality of life of individuals and families who had a solid plan to achieve their short- and long-term financial goals. They manifested their dreams and were able to do the things they had envisioned.

When it comes to building your financial house, it is the planning – not the hoping or mere dreaming – that actually turns your desires into realities. It is only through clearly-defined written goals, both measureable and time-bound, that you will realize the fruition of your dreams.

Typically, houses made of straw are built upon limited knowledge. For instance, a client of mine found herself $40,000 in credit card debt and bank loans. Her assets totaled a mere $13,000, leaving her with a deficit of $27,000. This client's financial house was built of straw, as she had little understanding of her debt or the steps required to reduce it. Houses made of wood are built upon slightly more knowledge, but the big picture is missing, and even though they may stand for a while, in the long run they rarely last.

However, houses made of brick are often built with the expertise of professionals who help them *evaluate* their dreams and *plan* the exact steps to attain their financial goals. I established clearly-defined and measurable actions for my client that would allow her to pay off her debts and achieve her goal to be financially independent. We started to plan and rebuild her financial house, only this time it was made of brick.

Laying the foundation of your financial house

A solid financial house starts with a strong foundation that can weather life's storms. The first step is to create a sound and solid financial plan. Alas, the harsh reality is that most people are ill-equipped to create a good plan. However, without one in place, there is a greater probability that your "house" will collapse when you need it most.

Start by writing down what you have, how much you make and what your goals are. These factors are essential to the planning process and should be incorporated within your financial plan. Other factors to consider that must be included are unexpected events such as job loss or even home loss.

Take the time to critically contemplate the lifestyle you wish to lead in your Golden Years of retirement and determine how much money you will need to live comfortably.

What rooms do you have in your house?

Building your rooms in your financial house is similar to the rooms built in your actual home. Just as you have rooms in your home that serve specific needs, such as a kitchen to store and preserve nourishment for you and your family, bedrooms to relax and rejuvenate your mind and body, an entertainment room to share laughs and play with your family and friends and bathrooms to refresh your personal hygiene, you have rooms in your financial house that serve specific goals. Yet, the rooms of your financial house must make sense and fit together properly into your overall financial plan.

Let's take a look at some possible rooms for your financial house.

☆ The Dream Room

What opportunities, career changes, and family developments do you hope to see in your lifetime? Your *Dream Room* captures your unique vision and your personal dreams. This room will help you understand yourself and your vision, as well as develop the necessary steps that reflect your dreams, both now and in the future.

☆ The Values Room

What values are most important to you? How would you like to impact the lives of others, your future generations? Your *Values Room* allows you to create a legacy for future generations.

☆ *The Lifestyle Room*

What are your tastes, your style of living? Your *Lifestyle Room* helps you define and prioritize your everyday desires through the process of addressing your budget and spending habits.

☆ *The Prosperity Room*

How do you define prosperity, your wealth? In your *Prosperity Room,* you will not only evaluate your net worth, but also your self-worth. You will develop a deeper understanding of the things that you have dedicated your time and energy to developing in your life.

☆ *The Economics Room*

Why would you take risks if you don't have to? Having an *Economics Room* helps you answer questions related to the economic risks that you are willing to take and how to communicate those risks. Your personality has an influence on your financial house and helps you to determine the types of investments best for you and your family's well-being.

☆ *The Children's Room*

How do you plan to help your children with their financial needs, without impacting your own? In your *Children's Room*, the focus is on your children's needs, from education to their inheritance. In this room, you will have "what ifs" to consider; long-term planning similar to retirement planning will be required.

☆ *The Retirement Room*

How fulfilling will your retirement be? In your *Retirement Room,* you will define your retirement timetable and identify how you will spend your life after work, while avoiding a shortage in finances.

☆ The Assets Room

Do you have relationships among family members, organizations or friends that you value? Working in conjunction with your *Assets Room* and *Prosperity Room*, you will evaluate these relationships and make certain to preserve your wealth for future generations.

Building a solid financial house is one of the most important things you can ever do for yourself and your family. The tale of *The Three Little Pigs* provides a perfect analogy for helping you gain a healthier perspective on the status of your current financial house, as well as helps you to clearly define where you are going, where you would like to be and how you are going to get there. To ensure that your financial house is in order, it is imperative that you gain a comprehensive financial education and acquire the skills, tools, and techniques necessary to understand and manage your finances. By improving your knowledge and making good use of available resources, you can create your financial plan, build your solid financial foundation and construct the financial house of your dreams with absolute confidence.

— ABOUT THE AUTHOR —

Pauline Bourne is a Financial Representative with Legacy Capital Group Inc. in Toronto, Ontario, with 30 years of experience in the life insurance industry. Her knowledge provides her clients with the tools they need to achieve financial independence. Pauline is the mother of two wonderful children, as well as a proud grandmother. When she is not helping her clients, she is involved in volunteer activities at her church, serving as Chair of the Ushers and Greeters, and a member of the advisory board. To obtain a copy of the Estate Planning Guide to ensure that your family and financial goals are met, visit her website at http://www.paulinebourne.com.

CHAPTER 18

Pathway to Greatness

Greg S. Reid

> *"Greatness is more than potential. It is the execution of that potential. Beyond the raw talent. You need the appropriate training. You need the discipline. You need the inspiration. You need the drive."*
> – Eric A. Burns

*E*ach one of us has greatness inside. Each one of us has the potential to play a bigger game, to become a better person, and to live a richer life. Yet, why do only so few achieve their goals? Why do most people settle for less? While all of us want to have the gold, not everybody knows the steps required and is willing to follow them. Gold doesn't come falling out of the sky and into your lap — you have to dig it out, and you will bump into obstacles before you'll be able to enjoy the fruits of your labor. Although your path will have obstacles, though, you have the choice to turn them into opportunities.

Let me share with you the five easy steps to achieve your goals:

1. **The easiest way to achieve a goal is to have one.** The first step is to know what you want. Many people have given up dreaming – or they

have a dream, but never set down the goals that will allow them to turn their dreams into reality. There is a saying, "For a sailor who doesn't know where he is going, every wind is unfavorable." You have to know at which harbor you want to dock, or else you may be floating on the ocean forever.

2 **A dream written down becomes a goal.** You can make your dreams come true when you have the courage and desire to pursue them. Get a journal and start writing down your dreams. Be creative, be spontaneous and have fun! When you have them in writing, you can read them over and over again. This will help to reinforce them in your mind. The next step is to break your dreams down into goals, and each goal into action steps. The action steps have to be scheduled on your calendar, and you have to be committed to do them—a plan backed by action will allow you to make your dreams come true.

3 **Stickability is the key to all great accomplishments.** Once you set your intentions on what you desire, stick to it— never let others (or yourself) talk you out of it before the miracle happens. So often, people work hard and long, making many sacrifices to achieve their goals, and what happens? They quit – they quit three feet from gold! Whenever you feel like giving up, remind yourself that you are only three feet from gold. All you have to do is keep going for a little longer, and all your efforts will pay off.

Build in yourself the confidence that you WILL achieve your goals. Sometimes it may take a little longer than you had expected, but don't allow that to discourage you. Having confidence will make you unstoppable in the attainment of your dreams. There is nothing as powerful as a positive mental attitude. Let go of your limiting beliefs and work on developing your attitude every day.

4   **There is no need to wait for the perfect circumstances.** So many people have great ideas and wonderful dreams. Yet, when asked why they don't follow through on them, they'll often say they are waiting for the perfect time to do it. They might say things like, "Well, once I find that perfect job…" or "Once I get some money saved up…" or "When the kids leave the house…" or "Once I find the right people to back me…" or whatever. Far too often, they allow outside chatter or their own negative self-talk to prevent them from taking action. Here's the big secret—there is *always* the perfect time to do something, and that time is *now*!

There are only so many hours in the day, only so many days in our lives on this wonderful planet. Make the most of them. Life's too short to wait it out; you can't get back the time you've already wasted. How many times have you waited too long only to have the opportunity vanish, or somebody else get credit for your idea? We all have something we've been putting off, a dream left unfulfilled in the hopes of finding "the right time." Sit down and figure out what it is that you've been waiting for, due to your own personal case of the "Once I's." Then just do it.

5   **It's the *Action* behind the *reAction* that really makes your dream come true.** Remember, you may have passion and you may have talent, but what good are they unless you follow through with action? *It's all about action.* You don't attract great things in your life by sitting on the couch, dreaming and hoping something wonderful will happen—you need to take action. If you want to meet the love of your life, what are the chances he (or she) will knock on your door while you are watching television, envisioning a wonderful person coming into your life? You want to visualize and then go out, meet new people and attract the right person.

You already know what excites you, so combine it with what you're good at doing—and then do something about it. Now is the time to separate yourself from the crowd of people who dream about success, and join the few that achieve it: Write down three simple tasks that will move you towards manifesting your dreams. When you wake up tomorrow, do those three things. Once completed, repeat the cycle and do it again. Yes, *it really is that easy.* Just like the adage goes, "A journey of a thousand miles begins with a single step." It's time to start moving—your dream is out there, waiting for you to get going. It's time to take the first step!

"Decide to live life to the fullest.
You may be three feet from gold."
— Napoleon Hill

— ABOUT THE AUTHOR —

 Greg S. Reid is a #1 best-selling author, filmmaker, motivational speaker, entrepreneur, and the CEO of several successful corporations who has dedicated his life to helping others achieve the ultimate fulfillment of living a life of purpose. Greg has been gifted the opportunity to follow in Napoleon's famous footsteps by sitting down with leaders of the day to discover how they persevered through challenging times; their stories are shared in *Three Feet from Gold*, a book he coauthored. He is a highly sought-after keynote speaker for corporations, universities and charitable organizations alike. www.alwaysgood.com

CHAPTER 19

Unleash the Forces of Nature Within

John B. Kemic

> *"Your moments will pass no matter what.
> Your strength lies in your ability to shape
> your moments. Your power lies in your ability to shape
> your moments with purpose."*

Sometimes the journey between where you are and where you want to be may seem overwhelming or even impossible, especially in those moments before you begin. It's taking that first step that somehow reveals the next one, then the next… until one day those smaller steps have brought you to your intended destination.

I first discovered this for myself over 20 years ago. I'd dreamed of seeing the Canadian Rocky Mountains from the moment I first saw them in a picture, but I was broke, unemployed and had no idea how to get there from where I was. All I knew, from something I'd read, was that *having* a specific goal leads to a better chance of *reaching* it. With that in mind, I took what steps I could to begin. I got a free brochure from a local motorcycle dealer, cut out the picture of the bike I wanted and pinned it to the wall. Beside that I pinned a calendar with a picture of the Rockies.

Each day I looked at those images, imagining the day I would crest some distant horizon on that motorcycle and see those mountains for myself. Somehow, things started falling into place. I got the job I needed, saved the money for the trip, bought the bike and — two years after pinning up those pictures – crested my distant horizon.

The seemingly ordinary act of pinning up a couple of images, was actually the first outward step toward an extraordinary experience that would change the course of my life. I'm pleased to share with you how you can take steps to do the same.

A power with which you were born

When the forces in nature are calm, we hardly notice them. On a still day it's easy to forget that you are living in a deep ocean of air. It's when air becomes movement in the form of wind, the focused force of a tornado or the sweeping mass of a hurricane that its presence makes itself known. That's the way it is with energy – it's through concentrated movement that its power is revealed.

Your thoughts are much the same way. You may not even notice them most of the time as you move through your daily life. Yet even at this moment you are using your thoughts – as naturally as you breathe – to read this. Your thoughts led to the actions that led you to read these words. You could have just as easily used your thoughts to instead go for coffee or spend time with family or watch TV or write a book or... or... or... And if you had, you'd be doing that instead.

So you see, your thoughts do guide your actions and your actions do produce your results. The question is, who's guiding your thoughts?

The trap of comfort

When you sit for a long time, you may occasionally shift your position. Why? Probably to get more comfortable. Usually, there's not much thought to this, just a reaction to an urge to feel more comfortable. That about sums up adulthood.

Growing up, you learned a series of urges to guide you toward comfort in your life. Those urges became a series of patterns. Those patterns became the guiding force behind your thoughts. Those patterned thoughts produce predictable actions which in turn produce predictable results which often lead to a well worn rut. To play an active role in guiding your thoughts, you must choose your focus rather than let your patterns choose for you.

The often overlooked forces within

The common, every day shopping list found on refrigerator doors all over, is a small scale example of choosing your focus.

This ordinary piece of paper holds your individual snippets of written intention ready to be acted upon when you go out into consumer heaven and, aisle by aisle, store by store, transform those snippets of intention into items in your cupboards, fridge and elsewhere around your home.

My friend, this is the essence of goal setting. You thought of something you wanted or needed, made note of it – giving it a place of importance in your mind – then took the steps to make it part of your life. Simple. Powerful. Effective.

If the ability to transform formless thought into substance in your cupboards is at your command, how far can you take this ability to shape the rest of your life? The answer lies in the things taken for granted all around you every day.

The large aircraft flying overhead, bridges, condos, houses, your car, your shoes, that handheld supercomputer known as a phone... all began in someone's mind as formless ideas. Those ideas, charged with purpose and intent, became goals. Those goals led to actions that shaped the fabric that makes up your known world. The goals that led to those results were set by people just like you, using the same ability you have – the same ability revealed by the simplicity of a shopping list.

You may not want to create large aircraft or buildings, but there may be things you do want to create – or change – in your life: finances, relationships, health, travel... something. You can use the power accessed by setting goals for whatever purpose you choose.

Gathering your inner forces

Goals give you an alternative to your familiar patterns. Alternatives create choice. It's by exercising your ability to choose an alternative of your own making, that you transform your thoughts from a light mental breeze into a focused, directed force of nature carving a path to your specific goal.

That's how your cell phone made the great journey from an idea in someone's mind to the useful object in your hand. And it's how you can shape your life once you decide the ways in which you intend to shape it.

Guiding your inner forces

☆ Set a goal. You don't have to know how you're going to get there. Start by choosing something, even if it's just setting a goal to have a goal.

☆ Write your goal down, put up a picture of it – do something to give it a presence outside of your thoughts.

☆ Choose a time frame within which to reach your goal.

☆ Keep your goal in mind by revisiting it every day.
    – Your familiar patterns of thinking come naturally. Thinking with a purpose in mind takes practice and persistence. So practice and persist. Imagine what you desire having already happened.

☆ Take action.

☆ Trust the process.

☆ Grab opportunities when they show up and take the next step as it's revealed.

☆ Be willing to receive the object of your goal when it arrives.

These steps may seem deceptively simple but the power you activate within yourself by taking them is anything but. When in doubt, just take out your handheld super computer phone and remember that it began its journey to your hand with these same basic steps.

Surprises along the way

Sometimes a goal really is about getting from point A to point B in the most efficient manner. There is value in setting sales goals, planning a vacation, aiming to buy that dream home – whatever it is for you – and then being happy with that result when you get there.   There may also be surprises along the way – surprises in the form of benefits over and above what you expected.

It's been over 20 years since I rode off into the sunset on that motorcycle. Though that motorcycle is long gone, the experience lingers – embers of a fire long gone out that still warms my spirit. The experience transcended a mere motorcycle or trip by also setting me on an inner road I didn't know would be part of the journey. I discovered my ability to make my goals a reality and my dreams come true while discovering more about myself along the way.

When you set a goal that seems beyond you, and you persist until you reach it, amazing and worthwhile experiences become possible, experiences that will stay with you well beyond the goal you originally set out for.

Your journey is far more than just the destination.   Start your memorable journey to your goal now by claiming your EXCLUSIVE audio 'Unleash the forces of nature within' and the companion action guide at www.checkpointpal.com/memorablejourney

— ABOUT THE AUTHOR —

 John B. Kemic is a co-founder of Checkpoint Pal™, a member based online community with the tools and support you need for reaching your goal in a fun and memorable way. As a speaker John delivers possibility, sharing personal experiences and leaving audiences with ideas and tools to change their lives. He reveals, through simple everyday examples, that we are all experts at creating results, and how to use that expertise to create the results we want. John is available for speaking engagements and can be contacted at john@checkpointpal.com. www.checkpointpal.com

CHAPTER 20

Cruising Your Way to Success

Larry Gruenwald

> *"Happy people plan actions, they don't plan results."*
> – Denis Waitley

id you have a big dream when you were young? Do you still have dreams you would like to come true? When you were young, that might have been all they were—dreams. How do you turn dreams into goals and goals into reality?

Over the years, I have applied certain principles to set and achieve many goals. I have a proven track record of turning around failing businesses, starting at the age of 24. I have successfully owned and operated many businesses, even up to four at one time. I either created them from the ground up or took over someone else's problem. I bought distressed retail businesses and through a combination of modernization to both their physical facilities and business practices, turned them around to profitability. One, for instance, went from a 10% profit margin to a 20% profit margin in less than 36 months. The real estate sales company I started generated within two years over 5 million dollars in sales— a 500% increase in business—and grew from 2 to 36 sales people. Many of the lessons that have helped me achieve great success I learned on my journey to Australia. Travel with me and I will share with you the steps I discovered on this incredible journey. The results of applying these steps could exceed your greatest expectations—they did for me.

When I was growing up, my dream was to become a cattle rancher. I was doing all the things needed to fulfill that dream. I started off in 4-H, a youth development organization, with projects that complement a ranch apprentice. Then, as high school came along, I was in FFA, a national organization dedicated to making a positive difference in the lives of students by developing their potential for premier leadership. While a member, I participated in all the projects and received several awards. I thought I was well on my way to achieving my dream when my family bought a larger ranch in Central Oregon and sold our ranch in Arizona. My mom put the ranch in my name, so there would be no inheritance taxes or disputes with my brothers when she passed away.

Unfortunately, the unexpected happened and I lost the ranch. Because the minimum age in Oregon to engage in a court proceeding is 21, I could not remove an old lien on the property, which was needed to sell the timber we had harvested. So we transferred ownership of the ranch back to my mom, with the understanding it was temporary. Sadly enough, she died before it was transferred back to me. All of a sudden, I had lost my mom, whom I loved so dearly, and I lost the ranch of my dreams. The ranch went into an estate, with other assets. In order for us to pay all the state (Arizona and Oregon) and federal taxes, we had to sell the property.

If unexpected situations come your way, you have to ask yourself "Do I hold on to my dream or do I dig deeper into my heart and ask 'What's next?'" Sometimes it's good to take a break and think things over, so I decided to go to Australia.

☆ Decide what you want and write it down

It's important to be clear on your goal and do your research so you can make good decisions and put your road map together. That's what I did. I wrote down my plan – I was going to take a ship to Australia and then take a road trip. I had $300 in my pocket, and I thought that would be enough since food was provided on the ship. Little did I know that instead of three months, I would be away for a full year.

☆ Write down how you are planning to achieve your goal

Finally, in March of 1967, at age 23, I left Los Angeles harbor on the *Monterey* cruise ship, with the first stop in Hawaii. The beautiful white beaches with turquoise water as far as you could see, good-looking Hawaiian girls dancing the hula and greeting us in a friendly manner and plants with leaves as big as elephant ears made me feel like I was in paradise. In my journal I had recorded the future I wanted to create, so my decisions, actions and thoughts would lead to the desired end. This was beyond anything I had imagined. No books I had read or movies I had seen about Hawaii could compare with this experience of a dream.

Just like in life, it is not only about getting to your destination (or achieving your goal), it is about the experiences you have on the way. In Bora Bora, I went diving in the Pacific wonderland—there were small and large fish of every color imaginable and the most amazing creatures. As I was living out this unbelievable experience I kept journaling to help me continue the process.

☆ Every experience is part of your trip

Tahiti—the real place of my dreams—was where the serendipity started and has continued ever since. Bert, an English writer who wrote a travel guide for Tahiti and the surrounding islands, introduced me to the owner of Criterion Music, who was there on vacation (the producer for Frank Sinatra). He encouraged me to participate in the local talent contest that a major hotel put on, and I won! This got me a job doing a number of evening performances in the "Bounty Club," which was a lot of fun. I stayed for a month in Tahiti and I had a great time. It taught me that it is ok to be flexible with my goals. I didn't lose sight of my goal of going to Australia, but I allowed myself more time to get there.

☆ Be flexible with your goal

When we docked in Sydney (Australia), this fellow from the BBC (British Broadcasting Corporation) named Tony Black boarded ship, looking for a story. One of the crew suggested talking to the American who played guitar and sang. So we had a chat. Then lo' and behold, he offered to let me share his flat and I didn't have to book a room.

Was this all in my plans? It was even better than I could have foreseen. As I was traveling longer than I had intended, I worked at gas stations, carwashes, any job to make money, even as a bouncer at a disco.

☆ Find people to help you who have the same goal

Despite all the great opportunities that came my way, my goal was to see Australia and I wanted to move on. I put a group together—one American, one Englishman, one Australian lady, and myself—who wanted to go to Western Australia, and we shared the expenses. I bought an old car and off we went to Perth.

☆ Do whatever it takes to achieve your goal

In Perth, I sold my share in the car and started hitchhiking around the country. I was so efficient, I could travel on about $20 per 1,000 miles. I made a figure eight around the whole country, working here and there. I drove a truck, worked as a laborer, whatever popped up.

☆ Be open to changes in your plan

All along the way, opportunities opened up, which made up a year that was so precious, I could never have even imagined it. After one year of incredible adventures, I made it home safely and still had $12.50 in my pocket. It wasn't always smooth sailing—eddies and storms happened along the way. That is how life is.

When you have a goal and live in the moment, you can manifest great things beyond your dreams. Don't let fear stop you from missing out on the great experiences life has to offer. Sometimes you may decide to let go of a dream and go in a different direction. I didn't become the rancher I had envisioned myself to be, but nevertheless, my life has been filled with new dreams I made come true.

Believe in yourself and know that you are a special person; there is only one of you in the entire world. Set your goal and follow your roadmap, while at the same time being open to unexpected possibilities. Keep your eye on the ball, and your dreams will manifest. Continue this process over and over in all areas of your life, and you will experience life as a never-ending adventure.

It would be my pleasure to help you achieve impressive results in your life and business. Feel free to contact me if you need help turning your business around. To start on your path of incredible success, go to www.Cruising2Success.com to get your copy of the "12 Step Method for Achieving your Goal," and use the password book4u.

— ABOUT THE AUTHOR —

Larry Gruenwald earned a B.A. in Psychology from Ottawa University in Phoenix, Arizona (4.0 GPA in all course work). He is a certified Seminar Leader with Financial Independence Network Limited, Inc., in Boscobel, Wisconsin on the topic of personal finance, with debt elimination as his specialty. Larry also has been trained in Communication and Team Building with Landmark Education. He is a Certified Business Coach with Eagle's View Systems, Inc., and a member of CoachLab International, a Society of Professional Coaches. When he is not working, Larry likes to go scuba diving or snow skiing. www.Cruising2Success.com

CHAPTER 21

What is Your End Game?

Jim Alvino

> *"In order to improve your game, you must study the endgame before everything else. For whereas the openings can be studied and mastered by themselves, the middle game and end game must be studied in relation to the end game."*
>
> — Jose Capablanca

*I*magine you are sitting in front of a chess master, and this is your first chess match ever. You are playing white, which means you make the first move. Thinking that the center of the board might get a little congested, you decide to get creative, take an oblique approach, and attack from the flank. Seven moves later, you're in checkmate!

This is the Fools Mate that can befall a neophyte for violating the principles of the game: ignoring the center of the board (in chess, you fight to control the center); moving the Queen, the most powerful piece on the board, or other heavy artillery out too soon or too frequently; leaving the King, the prize you are supposed to protect, vulnerable to attack or entrapment. Many entrepreneurs are playing this kind of opening with their enterprise, and they have no end game.

To achieve your goals in business, as in chess, a winning strategy is crucial. Timing and sequencing are important. Creating a successful strategy requires that you think differently. In a game of chess there is an opening, a mid-game, and an end-game. When we launch a business, it is common to charge ahead with energy, enthusiasm, optimism, and a heavy dose of blind faith. It is less common to know where we're going and usually unheard of to think about an end game. Just as in playing a game of chess, you need to look and think ahead to see potential scenarios. You have to think, assess and determine how different scenarios play out, how they might affect you, how you will respond, and where you can be proactive. This is how you will win your game of business.

When I founded Monetize Your Niche®, Inc. in 2009, I sought trademark protection. During the filing process, my attorney asked me a simple question: "What is your exit strategy?" I didn't have one. You may be in the same boat.

☆ Strategic Thinking

Once you become more familiar with the game of chess, you become more adept at strategizing and planning your moves ahead. It's the same in the game of business. Over the course of a 25-year career in the corporate world, as well as in association management, I was the top executive for four organizations, not including my own entrepreneurial ventures. In each case, our goal setting was guided by a strategic planning process which set clearly-defined and objective targets we called Quantifiable Measures of Success [QMS].

You will derive an Action Plan from these targets, 5 W's that detail WHO does WHAT by WHEN WITH WHAT [Resources]. The 5 W's indicate specific allocations of resources toward specific end games, set in advance. In a game of chess, each piece has a numerical value (e.g., pawn = 1, Queen = 10), and each has a capacity to make different kinds of moves. You might sacrifice a pawn, which can make very limited moves (usually one square at a time) to gain an advantage on a Rook or Castle with a numerical value of 5. In similar fashion, you might give away a lower-value product or service ("lost leader") with the goal being to inspire your customer or prospect to buy a higher-priced item.

Measurable targets, your Quantifiable Measures of Success, are the end points for a designated time frame (day, week, month, quarter, year, 3-5 years, etc.), and they dictate your daily actions. In short, you begin with the goal or end point in mind, and reverse-engineer your steps. As in a chess game, the sequence of strategies and tactical moves (your action steps) that lead to checkmating your opponent (attainment of your goal) is likely to change along the way; flexibility and creativity in the face of changing market conditions, circumstances, and opportunities are critical. But you still begin by visualizing the total picture, from start to finish.

Upon completing your annual (or more frequent) planning process, post a large chart of the 5-7 QMS you have established on the wall above your desk to serve as a:

- Visual reminder of your direction and goals
- Graphic benchmark of having hit a short-term or longer-term target
- Filter to stay focused

☆ Goal Set with Creative Problem Solving (CPS)

Apply a short decision-making protocol (oversimplified flowchart below) to determine the feasibility of an idea and whether it would take you closer or farther from your goals:

1. Does the new project or idea fall under one or more of the 5-7 QMS? If NO, end of discussion; if YES, under which one(s)?

2. Is the new project or idea an obvious Top Priority? If NO, it goes

to the back burner; if YES, is it equal to or greater than other Top Priorities under the specific QMS?

3. If NO, it goes to middle burner; if YES, a discussion ensues on Resources needed to incorporate the new project: the impact on your plan, budget, team, and the like.

4. Overall, how does this new move feel? Is it positive? Are there any red flags lurking in the unconscious urging you to address them? What is your "little voice" telling you? (As Donald Trump asks himself: "What am I pretending not to see?")

To assess the relevance and feasibility of a course of action taking you closer or farther from your goals, you can employ an objective, 6-step Creative Problem-Solving (CPS) process I learned from creativity pioneer E. Paul Torrance, in which you begin with a description of murky issues, identify an underlying problem, brainstorm multiple solutions, set evaluation criteria, evaluate the potential solutions, and arrive at one you determine to be the best. Among the key evaluation criteria is congruence with your company's values. Put the "best solution" to the same "feel right" test as you used in entertaining the new idea or project in the first place.

☆ Become the "Chess Master" of Your Entrepreneurial Niche

Many entrepreneurs become opportunity seekers, jumping from idea to idea, hoping something will stick and make an impact on their cash flow. To become the "chess master" of your entrepreneurial niche, you require an understanding of how the board is set up, how the game is played, and what constitutes an appropriate opening, mid game and end game. What will your foray into the marketplace look like? What business model will you adopt or adapt? Who is already successful in your niche that you might model, and how will you differentiate yourself from them? In a variety of scenarios, what might your expansion look like? How will you leverage what you do? (Email jim@monetizeyourniche.com to get your free report on Advanced Business Development.)

An exceptional entrepreneur, like a chess master, must be able to visualize several moves ahead, learn to anticipate and respond, be proactive yet flexible, offensive as well as defensive, take calculated risks, and execute his or her creativity within the parameters of the playing field.

A chess game is played for control and domination in the center of the board, usually not in the flanks. An entrepreneur needs to contend in the center of his world, too—both online and offline, equally—with a budgeted allocation of resources.

☆ The Elements of a Good End Game

Planning your end game might be the most significant goal-setting activity of your entire enterprise. Your end game will govern from the launch, through development and expansion, to eventually "handing over the keys" to someone else, in one form or another. And for you, this could be the equivalent of checkmate!

However, here is where we must leave our chess master behind, as he is forever a lone wolf; a good end game in business requires a maturity that transcends a founder's ego and a business model that is strictly person-dependent. A successful end game requires collaboration, ongoing coaching, often joint ventures, and a team approach, which may include a precise valuation of your business, depending on the actual exit strategy you are envisioning.

Re-conceptualizing my business model, having an exit strategy—an end game—has infused renewed energy into my day-to-day thinking and activity. Indeed, I am in the process of attracting all that I need to do, know and have to bring this goal about. What is your end game? Start planning it now!

To arrange a FREE webinar for your sales or management team on attracting more of what you want in your business and less of what you don't, email jim@jimalvino.com and type "Attract More Business" in the subject line.

"Helping entrepreneurs pursue their passion for profit."

— ABOUT THE AUTHOR —

James Alvino is the president and founder of Monetize Your Niche®, Inc. Jim is a dedicated coach and business consultant who is an expert at facilitating strategic planning and creative problem-solving. He is a published author, award-winning educational journalist, and endurance athlete, who applies his experience and wisdom in helping his clients fulfill their highest potential. Jim is the creator of "Secrets to Monetizing Your Niche" and its sequel, "Dominate Your Niche in 29 Days." Visit www.MonetizeYourNiche.com for these and other outstanding resources. jim@monetizeyourniche.com. © 2011 by James Alvino

CHAPTER 22

Stars of Dreams

Zenaida Roy-Almario

*I used to look up to the dark skies
To see the bright shimmering stars,
For there, occupied my many dreams
Hanging on the edges, so very far.
Until one night, I saw a star
Steadfastly fall down in a trailing blaze.
A dream of mine ran its final course
Tired of waiting for me to amaze.
My dreams kept me awake
For many nights and endless hours,
Until I wrote them all down
To fuel them with amazing powers.
My dreams are not meant to be
Locked inside my mind to be untold,
Writing my hopes, plans and goals
Was my start into making this a better world.*

– Zenaida Roy-Almario

*A*s a young adult, many hours of solitude were spent in the abyssal darkness of my room. Curtains were drawn tightly, as if aluminum foil lined the window panes, preventing the outside world from peeking at my most private thoughts. The door was locked. My fingers were always tightly gripping my pen as though I was in a panic to squeeze the last ink droplet onto my journal before fleeting thoughts of creativity dissipated into thin air, never to be captured again, their magic, beauty and definiteness. This was my dream world of being a famous author that I shared with no one. For no one could ever relate, understand or see the value of my dreams' possibilities. So I thought.

A dream is something you hope, desire and long for, that is usually perceived as difficult in nature or making come true. It is something that is so far removed from your present circumstance that it is too hard to imagine it as being possible, especially where other people are concerned. Some people have a fear of failing. Some people do not have dreams at all, nor do they dare to.

If you are not actively pursuing your hopes and dreams, it is because you have not been given the permission slip to have a definite purpose in life nor have you been informed of the BRAGN™ secrets to successful goal setting and achieving.

BRAGN™ secrets to successful goal setting and achieving:

1. Be A Big Dreamer
2. Resonate The Passion
3. Act, Creating Stepping Stones
4. Get Intentional Results
5. Nurture Your Belief

1 **Be A Big Dreamer!** Find a quiet place where you will not be interrupted, for some personal time. Pretend you are sitting on a "clean writing slate" that goes on as far as your eyes can see. Close your eyes. Breathe in slowly. Exhale slowly. Repeat a few more times until you are relaxed and focused. Imagine vividly and dream big, in multi-dimensions. This dream of yours—see it, hear it, smell it, taste it, touch it and be in it. Make it in the present tense, make it in the "now." If you could do anything as a profession, without any thought about educational cost, what would it be? See the people you are helping. See the difference you are making. How much money are you making a year? How much money will you have in your savings account? What kind of car are you driving? Where are you vacationing? What does your house look like? How big is your house?

Okay, you have just been "put on notice" as to how to dream big and in living color. You have been formally given the permission slip to dream. Nothing is impossible if you put your mind, heart and soul into making your dreams come true, especially if it involves providing service to the world around you.

Maintain a dream journal. It's a proactive way to focus on your visions, dreams and goals. By clearly defining and re-reviewing them in your own words, you take ownership and create feelings of attachment and passion for them. It fuels you to take action. Include photos in your journal. Journaling creates a commitment, on your part, to see your dreams come true! You are also informing your Higher Being and the Universe of what it is you desire and want. When you clearly define your desires, the message goes out and sets in motion exactly what is needed to physically match the vibrations of your thoughts and intentions, to make your visions, dreams and goals come true. When your thoughts are clear, it is easy for your Higher Being and the Universe to respond accordingly.

2 **Resonate *The Passion* of your dream, from your head to your toes!** When you decide on your ultimate big dream, you will find yourself to be passionately excited! It will consume you. It will keep you

awake into the wee hours of the night, until you fuel it with amazing powers, through your journaling. You will want to share with everyone your ideas that tie perfectly into your ultimate big dream. Hearing and seeing you share your dream passionately, your Higher Being and the Universe will present opportunities and send people your way purposefully, never coincidentally.

3 *Act, Creating Stepping Stones* **that will pave the path to your ultimate big dream.** At the top of your journal, write your dream in a positive statement. For example, in writing my first book, my ultimate big dream and goal was, "From our launch date until December 31, 2011 BRAGN™ – Be Real And Great Now will inspire ten million young adults."

Below your goal statement, write the numbers one through thirty. Next to each number, write out action steps that will help you reach your ultimate dream goal. These become your "mini goals" that will lead you to your ultimate dream goal. Prioritize these thirty goals according to their importance and how they contribute to your ultimate dream goal. Be sure to include goal dates next to them. Keep in mind that these goal dates are not set in stone. If you miss the date on a mini goal, do not worry; simply review and redefine it and re-set the date. Never change your main goal. You can further clarify it and adjust the date. Don't ever feel the pressure or need to give up on your goal(s). Your moment to shine will arrive, when your Higher Being and the Universe know that you are ready to receive it.

4 *Get Intentional Results* **to come your way by following the first three secrets mentioned above.** When you decide what your ultimate dream goal is, and you are passionately and emotionally involved in making it come true and taking action steps toward it, you will be amazed at the process that starts to unfold in manifesting your heart's

desire! You will start to experience what you will initially believe as things that are coincidental. However, you will realize that they are actually intentional results! Intentional results, because you clarified and were proactive in creating your ultimate dream goal and took stepping stones towards its reality!

5 *Nurture Your Belief* in yourself! You will have people come into your presence that will wholeheartedly believe in you and your ultimate dream goal, however, they are fewer than the ones that will not. It is okay! You see, your Higher Being and the Universe gave you this vision and ultimate dream goal. Only you can do this vision and ultimate dream goal justice. No one else can, which is why others cannot be as passionate about it as you. It is okay! Write out a list of positive affirmations that tie into making every action stepping stone possible and making your ultimate dream goal a reality. Affirmations like, "I am a goal achiever," and "I have special gifts and talents that will provide value to the world." Make it a priority to be your number one fan, always! You are a goal achiever!

Thoughts are things, and they are powerful. When your thoughts connect with your passion and desires in life, amazing dreams are created. When your dreams are translated into words and pictures, definite plans for them to manifest are in motion and it is necessary to take action. Your actions are stepping stones towards achieving your goals and turning your dreams into realities. I know because today, as an author, people relate, understand and value my dreams' possibilities to inspire and motivate young adults everywhere. It is my mission to encourage, inspire and guide young adults to Get BRAGN™ - Be Real And Great Now, and increase their lives' positive results!

Be inspired to dream big and get your FREE book chapter, "BRAGN™ To Make It Happen." Send an email to zenaida@berealandgreatnow.com, subject line: FREE Chapter.

— ABOUT THE AUTHOR —

Zenaida Roy-Almario is a youth motivator, mentor and author of BRAGN™ – Be Real And Great Now. Zenaida provides empowering communication skills that young adults can utilize today, to spare them trials and heartaches. Zenaida has an Associate Arts degree in Communications Studies. She also studied various communication programs. For speaking engagements and more information on BRAGN™, please visit www.berealandgreatnow.com.

CHAPTER 23

Boot Camp Strategies for Life

Mark Rabbitt

> *"Character—the willingness to accept responsibility*
> *for one's own life—is the source from which*
> *self-respect springs."*
> – Joan Didion

The experience was intense—the anticipation and anxiety, coupled with the fear and self-doubt—all merged. Kids from all over the United States were waiting at the airport for the bus to the Marine Corps Recruit Depot, in San Diego. A tall man appeared, directing us with a deep voice to gather our belongings and get on the bus. "Heads down, no talking, and absolutely no moving around!" were the instructions bellowed from a small, yet very compact, gentleman at the front of the bus. These two men were clean cut and very direct. Their expectations were communicated clearly. Their uniforms were immaculate—sharp creases in their shirts and trousers—and their shoes were clean and shiny.

This has been an awesome visual picture that I have maintained throughout my journey through Marine Corps Boot Camp . . . and through life. Over the years, I've come to appreciate how valuable the lessons were that I learned in the Marine Corps, first as a recruit, and later as a Drill Instructor, because they build the character you need to be successful in life.

Join me for a day at the Marine Corps and discover the boot camp strategy for life that will help you achieve any goal you want.

When the alarm goes off at 4:00 am, I want to roll over and hit the snooze button; unfortunately this is not a luxury a Marine Corps Drill Instructor has in life. Even though I didn't get to bed till 11:45 pm, I have an hour's drive ahead of me, as the drill instructors must be on deck by 5:15 am, before the recruits wake up at 5:30 am.

The core values of Honor, Courage, and Commitment help forge the spirit of every Marine. This is accomplished by the example the Drill Instructors set on a daily basis. They say that a company can be as good as the leadership, because the integrity and the character of the business owner will reflect throughout the company. Leadership is developed by taking action and setting the example that others want to follow.

In order for you to become a good leader, not only in your company, but also in your personal life, you want to build your character with these core values:

Honor:

☆ Honor yourself by having a vision for your life. What is your purpose? What do you want to achieve? Don't let fear hold you back from having a big dream and working every day to become a better you.

☆ Keep your word. When you keep your word, people will know they can count on you, they will trust you and this will strengthen the relationship with your clients, your family and your friends. Keep your word to yourself, because if you don't, this can slowly break down your self-confidence, as you'll start to doubt yourself.

No matter how tired I am when the alarm goes off, there is no question in my mind whether I'm getting up or not—the recruits are counting on me. When it's just you, it's easy to hit the snooze button and sleep in for a little longer, but you can't do that when you have others to hold you accountable.

☆ Take responsibility for yourself and your actions. When you didn't do as well as you expected or made a mistake, don't blame others. Analyze what you can do differently and learn from the experience.

☆ Respect others. Every human deserves to be treated with respect and dignity, regardless of their ethnic or social background. When you do this, others will, in return, treat you with respect.

☆ Don't settle for your best. With continued training and refinement of technique, your best today will be overshadowed by your best tomorrow!

As I drive to work, I think back on the day that the bus picked us up from the airport to go to the Marine Corps Recruit Depot. My instructors certainly helped me to grow by not allowing me to settle. By working hard, I now am one of those instructors, teaching the new recruits to be better every day. Yesterday, we planned everything out. We know the schedule from the moment we get started till the lights go off at 9.30 pm. Today, we have a heavy physical program. It is important that the recruits are in an excellent shape. Physical fitness is the first measure of success and a well-conditioned Marine has more energy, mental clarity and a stronger will to succeed.

Courage:

☆ It takes courage to have big goals. Some may be afraid to do what they really want; because they are afraid they might fail.

☆ Do the right thing because it is the right thing to do, even if it's not the popular thing to do.

☆ Don't make excuses. Quitting is not an option.

☆ Overcome your fears by taking action.

This morning, we have the recruits jump off the rappel tower. I can see the fear in the green eyes of the young man. I feel for him, because it reminds me of my own experience. I had a terrible fear of heights. While I was almost frozen from fear on the edge of that rappel tower, once I took the first step — leaning back off the edge of the tower — a sense of peace, freedom and an excitement charged through my body. I yelled, "On rappel!" and the Marine on the ground yelled, "On belay!" I bounced off the ledge of the tower and with three more bounces down the tower, I was on the ground, running. It was a valuable lesson, because it showed that often things are not as bad as we imagine them in our heads. The more often you do what frightens you, the less nervous you are. Whether this is making sales calls, speaking on a stage, or jumping off rappel towers, the only way to overcome your fear is by taking action and doing it, anyway, regardless of how you feel.

Commitment:

☆ Be committed to others and to yourself. Be committed to sharpen your skills and become a professional.

☆ Have discipline. It's been said you either pay the price of discipline, which weighs ounces, or you pay the price of regret, which weighs tons. The choice is yours… either way, you are going to pay a price.

☆ Get it done. It doesn't matter what you have going on in your life. It's up to you to make the changes you want!

Even though the training program is tough, the recruits push themselves. Nobody wants to be the loser of the team. Often we create limitations of what we can do in our minds, but I've come to discover that humans are often capable of much more than they realize. I see this happen every day. They are exhausted and think they can't make it, but the peer pressure is so strong, they refuse to give up and exceed their expectations. In life, it is critical to select our peers carefully, because they will affect our performance. Do your peers encourage you to go beyond your imagined boundaries?

✩ Follow through on your plan. The implementation of a well thought out action plan will determine your success. Your results depend on the amount of daily focused activities you perform, on a consistent basis.

In the evening, we review our day and make our plan for the next day. I have been up and running for almost 18 hours, today; time to go home, get four to five hours sleep and provide another day of training, tomorrow. Excellence doesn't happen by accident: It requires honor, courage and commitment. It has to be developed every day, so it becomes a part of your being. Training and committed practice will allow you to perform at your highest level.

After teaching, coaching and leading over 20,000 Marines, I know that the principles I have shared with you in this chapter will build your character and can make you unstoppable in reaching your goals. You may be surprised to discover what you are capable of accomplishing. My goal is to inspire you to *Step into Your Vision*. You are in control of your life; don't give your power away! As a Human Performance Specialist, I can help you focus and develop your potential to create the life you want. Life is full of amazing moments—enjoy them all! Have fun and feel free to live the life of your dreams!

Claim your free mini Boot Camp '52 Weeks to Leadership' at www.markrabbitt.com/bookspecial.

Inspiring All Those Who Aspire To Greatness
Within Themselves

— ABOUT THE AUTHOR —

Mark Rabbitt is a Human Performance Specialist with over 22 years of leadership experience—from Leadership Consultant, Equal Opportunity Advisor, and Department of Defense Mediator, to Team-Building Facilitator. In the Marine Corps, Mark played a significant role in creating the kind of environment where everybody has an equal opportunity to achieve their personal and professional goals. He now uses the principles he taught as a Marine Corps Drill Instructor and Martial Arts Instructor to help others create a better life for themselves and their families. www.markrabbitt.com

CHAPTER 24

Your Road Map for Life

JoAnn Oppenheimer

> *"If you don't know where you are going,*
> *How do you know when you have arrived?"*

*a*s we mature, we become more aware of where we have been and where we are. We may look back at our lives and ponder the choices and decisions we made along the road. When we were young, our parents may have suggested a path that they thought we should take. Some of us listened and did just that. Others were not satisfied with the path they were shown. They did not want to live a rubber-stamped life like their parents or siblings. They wanted to march to a different drummer and follow their own dreams.

Where are you today? Have you been true to yourself? Have you arrived at where you want to be?

Maybe you are single again—here you sit at the dining room table, by yourself. This is probably not where you envisioned yourself to be. Whether you have lost your partner due to a death, divorce or a breakup, we all go through the grieving process—the shock, the denial, the terrible

155

sadness and loneliness. It can be a challenge to start this new chapter in your life. It can be extremely painful or it can be freeing and empowering, depending on the circumstances and how you choose to deal with it. You can choose to make adjustments and find happiness again or be miserable for the rest of your life.

Because of my own personal experiences of going through three divorces and the death of my last husband, I have learned valuable lessons I would like to share with you and support you in your transition to becoming single again. There may be uncertainties and fears that you are facing. Asking for help and guidance can make the difference in the life that you are seeking.

When you have lost your mate, the first step is to explore who you are without him or her. You'll need to find your direction in life again, and create a plan or Road Map that will get you from where you are to where you want to be. Road Maps are needed in all areas of life and are the key to happiness and achieving your goals.

Between my junior and senior years of college, I got married for the second time. Unfortunately, after 15 years of marriage, I became a single mother of two children. We lived in a beautiful home, and my children were able to participate in many extracurricular activities because my business income afforded us the ability to live an upper middle class life. This was made possible by setting goals, staying focused and working hard. Because I was the one who wanted the divorce, I felt free and finally at peace.

I always found fulfillment in working and running my own businesses. On my own, I no longer was accountable to another person for having to explain who I was doing business with or how I was spending my money, and was able to make my own decisions. My ex-husband was from Russia and had thought it was embarrassing to have a working wife. He hadn't even been able to admit to our friends that I worked full-time and contributed to our financial household.

My last husband was everything I had looked for in a mate, and I was devastated that he became terminally ill 15 months after we married. I missed the life we had before his illness, but he taught me what *pure love* is. Being married for less than five years and his caretaker to the end, I had already begun the mourning process along the way. After his death, I faced each day with an ability to cope, a positive mental attitude, and being content with my status of being single again. Being a widow instead of a divorcee that time, I soon realized that people look at you differently when you are a widow. Another of life's lessons was learned. No matter if the loss of a mate is through a breakup, divorce, or death, coping and continuing to live your life takes work and direction to go where you want to go.

I now take these lessons I've learned in life to help newly single people build what I refer to as Road Maps to get from Point A to Point B, through my "Single Again?" coaching. Road Maps are essential to stay on course and arrive at the desired destination. Each person must decide what the right path is for them. This is very important in order to achieve tranquility and peace of mind.

☆ Nurture your relationships

A high priority on your Road Map is to continue to nurture your personal relationships with family, friends and business associates. Keep in touch, recognize others on special occasions (or for no reason at all), and set a goal always to be a thoughtful person. It is crucial to continue interacting with those in your inner circle.

☆ Build your self-esteem and positive attitude

Two of the greatest emotional states you can experience are self-confidence and a positive mental attitude. Don't let the elements of uncertainty, instability, and frustration affect your mental and physical health, negatively.

☆ Handle your finances

When you are at a loss wondering how you'll pay your bills or feel overwhelmed with balancing the books because your mate took care of them, find somebody you trust who can help you. Put your house in order and include this on your Road Map, as well. Ask a friend, a family member or seek out entities that offer services to teach how to handle personal finances or can refer you to low-cost or free professional service providers.

☆ Plan your work and work your plan

What does this mean? Make a list pertaining to a category of goals and number each one, in order of the highest priority to the lowest. As you reach each goal, remove it from the list. You need to have long-term and short-term goals for your Road Map: Where do you want to be in the future? Set deadlines and determine the action steps to accomplish these goals. Some goals may take years to complete. In that case, you must break it down into smaller sub-goals. Write the goal and sub-goals on their own lists. Then add these goals, a few at a time, to your daily Road Map. Eventually, you will complete all the sub-goals, thus accomplishing the main goal you originally were determined to reach.

☆ Make lemonade

"When life hands you lemons, make lemonade." In other words, you must learn to cope with the twists and turns life brings. Keep in mind that "a positive mental attitude affects your altitude." Be aware that not all Road Maps will bring you to your intended destination, but they sometimes open doors to greater opportunities. Some of the best things that happened to me took place when they were least expected. We cannot look into a crystal ball to predict the future, as unexpected bumps in the road can and most likely will occur. You may decide to go in another direction due to an unexpected opportunity, or your plate may have been too full at that time. Keep your life fulfilling by always setting new and exciting goals.

☆ *Make new friends*

Go to places where people you meet have like interests, such as the gathering places of local professional groups, dancing venues, museums, galleries, adult education classes, ski clubs, concerts and book clubs. Be adventurous! Some singles think they should no longer retain social relationships with married friends because they are now single. This is absolutely untrue! Continue to invite couples to your home for cookouts and parties so that they, too, will keep you on their guest lists. Remember married people know other single people whom they could introduce you to. If you have a partner, they will accept you bringing this person with permission, of course. If you do not have someone, go alone and enjoy your friends.

Through my own personal experiences of divorce, breakups, and widowhood, I have learned that there is a need to build a Road Map for Life, which provides guidance and support during the transition into the "Single Again?" lifestyle. This new chapter in your life can be full of uncertainties and fears, but with my help and the help of others, you can move forward down the road in a positive direction.

My gift to you is a FREE 15 minute coaching session, over the telephone, to help you with your transition from couple to "Single Again." E-mail me at JoAnn@CoachSingleAgainAt50Plus.com to schedule an appointment.

— ABOUT THE AUTHOR —

An Entrepreneur, Realtor, Author, and Coach, JoAnn Oppenheimer has been a successful business woman for over 50 years. At this point in her life, her primary focus is helping people navigate through personal and business issues they face on a daily basis. JoAnn is a published author and columnist coaching men and women through their transition from couple to "Single Again? at 50+." She is available for public speaking engagements, radio and television interviews, and private coaching. JoAnn may be reached at JoAnn@CoachSingleAgainAt50Plus.com. www.CoachSingleAgainAt50Plus.com

CHAPTER 25

Love, Win, Live
Turn Your Challenge into an
Opportunity

Samira Bachir

> *"Be the change you want to see in the world."*
> – Mahatma Ghandi

*I*t was late when I landed at the airport in Montreal. My business trip to Toronto had been very successful, and I was happy to be home again. There was a voice message from an ER doctor at the Hotel Dieu Hospital, which said, "Ms. Bachir, please come directly to the emergency room as soon as you get this message. We have detected an anomaly in your X-rays." Even though I didn't exactly understand what it meant, I knew something was really wrong, so I got in the car and quickly drove to the hospital.

After several days of intensive tests, a pulmonologist brought me into his office and said, "Samira, I am sorry to tell you, but you have non-Hodgkin lymphoma in the thymus. It is not operable. If you take the treatments, you have a 50/50 chance of success; if you don't, you will have about six months to live."

All I heard after that were distorted words spoken in slow motion. Nothing made sense anymore. It was as if I had been instantly transported into another dimension. There I was at 42, facing a death sentence.

The hardest part was telling my two sons and my mom what I was facing. It was heartbreaking. I felt that I was inadequate and a disappointment as a daughter and a mom. I just could not believe what was happening. My mom, who has now passed away, was very ill at the time. My sons, whom I had raised on my own, had no emotional outlet, nor anyone else to turn to, and I was too weak to support them through this difficult journey we were all facing. It was a big challenge. I had no clue as to how I could win the battle with cancer, but I was not willing to give up—and neither should you.

When you start your own business, you have no idea what life is going to throw at you either, but you have to decide that no matter what happens you will never give up. You have to be flexible and creative in finding solutions for the challenges that you will face in life and in business.

☆ Set your intention to win!

Your success depends on you. Know what you want and fill your life with it. Just keep moving forward and figure it out from there. You don't need to have it all mapped out. What will make a huge difference are the people you surround yourself with. Stay away from negativity and stay away from negative people. Decide to succeed. Don't be afraid of success or failure. You will be hit, but you can get back up again. It's not always easy, but MAGIC happens when you are able to stay focused on your vision. See, feel and taste your goals, even if you don't have a plan all mapped out yet.

☆ Always remember your WHY

When moving forward is very difficult, don't let the emotions of the moment overwhelm you and take you down. Focus on why you want to achieve your goal. Why is it so important to you? How will you feel once you have achieved your goal?

Often, I cried myself to sleep at night. I was afraid and felt as if I was fighting an invisible giant. After the treatments, I felt like I had gone to hell and back. Sometimes I wanted to park my body somewhere and buy another one, because it was my body that was sick, not me. After my third round of chemo, I was very sick and everything seemed surreal. I did not know how I would ever finish the treatments. There was no way I could tolerate just one more treatment; I just wanted to forget about the rest of it. . . I was ready to give up dying seemed an easy way out... That is when I decided to stop all chemo rounds; after all, it was my decision to make. The pain was unbearable and so I did nothing for about 15 minutes until I felt a different kind of pain. A pain I had never experienced before, it was the fear of never seeing my boys again. I was not afraid of dying, but just not yet and not like this. I realised that I had let my pain and fear distract me from my goal. That is when I committed again to my goal and did not give up on myself. I wanted to have a level 10 relationship with my sons so badly that I didn't allow anything to stop me—I just had to win. I wanted to LIVE!

☆ Give yourself permission

Life is precious. You don't know when it will be taken away from you. Happiness is your birthright. Give yourself permission to live your dreams. All my life, I had done what I was expected to do: I was a good daughter, a good sister, a good mom, a good wife (I had even married the man my parents had chosen for me). One day, I realized that I didn't have to wait for somebody to tell me what to do or give me permission to dream and have goals. It was ok to do things for me and to think for myself. No matter what family you are born into or what cards you are dealt, you can decide to transform yourself and decide what you want to create in your life.

☆ *Learn to adapt*

A rocket on its way to the moon is only following the designated course 5% of the time—the other 95% of the time, it is continuously changing and adapting. Our society is moving rapidly – technology and marketing are changing as we are speaking. To be successful in reaching your destination or achieving your goals, you have to adapt to the continuously changing world around you without losing sight of who you are and where you are going.

My daily activities consisted of going from the couch to the bedroom and back again. Something inside me felt broken, but when I expressed the physical pain I was in or shared that I had difficulties in accepting my condition, the doctors would only increase my medications. That is when I turned to alternative medicine and kept searching to find what worked.

☆ *Think outside the box*

Embrace what you do well and surround yourself with the right people to create leverage and supply the elements you may not have— money, time and/or expertise. Ask for help. Be creative. If you can't afford to pay for someone's services, ask if you can help them by offering your strength. Be willing to give as much or more as you are willing to receive. You can train yourself to turn every challenge into an opportunity. Because I trained my brain to find creative ways to get out of a bad situation— whether health-, relationship- or business-related—I now see many possibilities everywhere, and I provide this brainstorming skill to business owners to help them when they are stuck or looking for creative ideas to expand their thinking.

☆ *Walk in faith*

To achieve your goals, you need to walk in faith and not in fear. Yes, you may make mistakes, trust the wrong people, lose money, but the most important thing is to always pick yourself up again, learn from your mistakes and never give up. Trust and take action. Don't be a sitting duck—keep moving. One of the lessons I learned was that the sooner I got out of my way I immediately discovered the hidden gift in the challenge, and the sooner life would then move me on to the next gift. Knowing that I had already overcome certain challenges in the past gives me the confidence that I have the tools to do it again – and so should you.

In life, there is no such thing as maintaining the status quo—there is growth or decay. Every challenge gives you the opportunity to grow. Transform yourself into the person you need to be in order to live the life you envisioned, no matter what life may throw in your path.

My journey has taught me many valuable lessons. I share those lessons to inspire, motivate and help others to take a stand in life, go beyond their limitations and break down the barriers that prevent them from achieving their goals. When you have challenging days, know that they will pass. Close your office and do something nice for yourself. Email me at efi@comf5.com and I will send you a free video to inspire you to "Embrace challenging days."

— ABOUT THE AUTHOR —

Samira Bachir graduated from McGill University in Public Relations Management. She helps entrepreneurs develop their businesses with her out-of-the box strategies, her life experience and her e-marketing tools. She loves to speak at events, teaching small and medium businesses how to use technology to increase their visibility and humanize their communications. You can reach Samira at 450-534-5547 or email her at efi@comf5.com.

Wings of Courage

You are expanding
Your mind and independence,
As life provides you with
More day to day experience.

You want to be the one
To pick out your best friends,
Create your own style
That awe and transcends.

Find your love interest
To create a special relation,
For undivided love
And dedicated attention.

Try new things to
Showcase your many talents,
And make lasting memories
Of distinctive moments.

It is exciting to see you
Spread your wings of courage,
Fly through each challenge
And never be discouraged.

- Zenaida Roy-Almario

CHAPTER 26

Power Achievement Secrets

David Braun

> *"Being an achiever is not enough, unless what that means is that we are benefiting other people."*
> – John Maxwell

Have you ever seen or been in a speedboat going very fast? Imagine yourself in one right now, at the wheel, going 50 miles per hour across the ocean. You hear the roar of the engines as its blades carve up the water at an incredible rate. Your hat is tied securely around your head and neck to keep it from flying off due to the intense wind. You feel the salty ocean spray prick your skin, and you see it spot your sunglasses, almost obscuring your view. And as you peer through them, you realize that instead of getting closer to your destination, you're getting farther and farther away. So you decide you must make a change in your course.

But what do you do? Do you nod your head up and down? Jog in place? Yell at another person in the boat to do something? No, none of those actions are effective. But notice that all of them are changes in your activity. They may be positive, well-intentioned, and you may be doing them very fast. Yet they will not, cannot yield the results you are seeking.

It is not until you take the ONE course of action, the correct one, which in this case is to make a *slight* turn of the steering wheel, that you will eventually reach your desired destination. Changing course too fast could capsize your boat! And it is the same with goal setting—you just need to make that ONE change.

Unfortunately, that ONE change may be difficult to determine since, as achievers, we lead very hectic lives. It can be exhausting just to take care of the kids, the house, the spouse, the job, etc. You may be hoping to find that ONE secret or that ONE aspect of goal setting and achieving that you can put in your arsenal to get you to your destination. You will get TWO in this chapter.

The First Power Secret: Achieve Your Goal, and Receive Your Rewards through Service

Think of the great achievers: Mother Teresa, Oprah Winfrey, Abraham Lincoln, Martin Luther King, etc. They shared one distinct ingredient in their accomplishments: service to others. If I have a goal I want to achieve, and it requires that I go beyond my current survival level, I must have a reason to accomplish it. You need a "Why that makes you cry." Your emotions must be a part of your why, and they need to be strong enough to make you think, "If I don't succeed, I'll cry." But if you have a goal that involves just you and nobody else, will you cry if you don't achieve it? For example, I may want to earn my MBA – but if I don't get it, will I cry? I may be disappointed, but I won't be heading for the tissue box anytime soon.

Initially, you feel great when you envision the life you want to create. However, the excitement can fade quickly when difficulties arise or the reality sinks in that hard work and sacrifice are needed. When this happens, you may want to abandon your goal, especially if you don't have one that deeply engages you. It's easy to get addicted to the drug of emotional adrenaline, not sticking to doing the often mundane, humdrum (but necessary) tasks, or facing the pain of obstacles and setbacks.

Sacrifice, doing what it takes, and *doing for others* is a huge part of a why that makes you cry—someone's life may literally depend upon what you do. Now recall the mission you have for your business and/or your life. Does it have an element of service in it? Here are some examples of great missions:

1. Jim Alvino's mission: "*Helping* entrepreneurs pursue *their* passion for profit."

2. Norma Kamali, an award-winning fashion designer and giant in the fashion world, says, "I use fashion to *help* women gain self-esteem."

> *"For even the Son of Man did not come*
> *to be served, but to serve. . ."*
> – Matthew 20:28

Most high achievers have a mission that fuels them, drives them, and sustains them. So look at your goals and ask yourself how accomplishing each one of them will serve others. Look back at a goal you didn't achieve—was it only about yourself? If you were to re-frame and make it about service to others, would it re-energize you? Would your goal become more achievable, and ultimately, more satisfying?

Even if you have your Why, with the ingredient of serving others, you might feel stuck, or "Life" just gets in the way. What can you do? David Byrd (from Paul J. Meyer at the Leadership Management Institute) says, "To be a goal achiever, you must be prepared to make effective choices on a daily basis." What are effective choices? Choices that relate to and move you forward in accomplishing your goals and dreams. It is critical to move from doing 80% situational activities and 20% goal-achieving activities to 20% situational and 80% goal-achieving activities. In order to accomplish this, you must become better at making more effective choices with your time on a daily basis. How?

The Second Power Secret: The Customizable Achievement Notebook

You probably know the importance of planning your days, weeks, and months ahead of time, but time gets filled up so quickly. You need a system tailored to your goals, dreams, and life, so you are crystal clear where you want to put your attention, energy, and focus. For me, it works great to split my to-do list into two sections: "Business to-dos" and "Personal to-dos." This allows me to focus on my Business items when I'm at work. Then when I am home, I can concentrate fully on my Personal items. I thought to myself, "Wow, this is great! Everyone should do this!" until I talked to my wife, Cheryl. She did not need a Personal to-do list. All she needed was a to-do list for her work. So that is what she is using today and it is working perfectly for her. But I needed more, and I took my "split-screen" notebook even further. I added a notes section for Business, and one for Personal, plus sections for my goals, vision, calendar, communications with others, monthly and weekly reviews, etc.

> *"There is nothing with which every man is so afraid*
> *as getting to know how enormously much he is capable*
> *of doing and becoming."*
> – Soren Kierkegaard, Nineteenth Century Danish philosopher

It's All About Realizing Your Highest Potential

All of us have huge potential to accomplish our goals. Most people start; unfortunately, only a few finish. Does this happen to you? It certainly has happened to me, but by using these principles, and by expanding the notion of planning and the functionality of conventional planners, I have become much more effective in achieving my goals.

Remember our speedboat? It is not the big shifts in our lives; it is the little changes that will make the big differences. Maybe your Why isn't strong enough yet, as perhaps you are focusing too much on yourself and not enough on your *service* to others. Or maybe you simply need a tweak in how you plan your daily actions, *customizing* your planning system to suit your needs now, with the ability to change when your life changes.

Why not start now by visiting my website and downloading my free document, "Creating Your 90-day Blueprint for Success," and achievement notebook templates, at www.proappcreators.com/freenotebook to begin to create significant changes in your life.

You are reading this book, this chapter, because you are an achiever – someone who doesn't want to settle for less than what you feel you can achieve. Today, right now, begin putting these concepts into practice. You have just one life: use your time wisely on a daily basis, and use it to serve others. Life is too short to do things any other way.

— ABOUT THE AUTHOR —

 David Braun is president and CEO of Pro App Creators, whose mission is to create innovative applications that bring life to mobile devices, helping people to change their lives. He is an avid student of goal setting and achieving, and loves to help educate people in this area. He offers training materials for goal setting and creating your own achievement notebook at http://www.achievement notebook.com/ as well as mobile applications that can enhance your productivity, while allowing you to tailor the experience to your needs. You may contact him at david.braun@proappcreators.com.

CHAPTER 27

Quantum Thinking for Success
Elizabeth Macarthur

> *"Nothing in life has any meaning*
> *except the meaning you give it."*
> — Tony Robbins

*L*ife is meant to be lived from a place of abundance, from which you achieve your goals and create amazing results. What is it that is holding so many of us back? What causes us to set wonderful goals, but struggle to achieve them? It is all that stuff that goes on in our heads and our thinking processes which we are most often not aware of. Are you willing to explore what is standing in your way? Are you open to making a shift?

The Skinny On Negativity:

Negative thoughts and feelings stop the flow of abundance. They stop the flow of positive results and can stop you dead in your tracks, far from reaching your dreams. Negative thoughts prevent you from taking the necessary actions to do what you know you need to do in order to achieve your goals. Emotions like resentment, judgment, anger and resistance are very disempowering and can also stop the flow of abundance, thus creating more roadblocks for you. These emotions can stay with you for a long time and prevent you from achieving the goals you want to attain.

Negative feelings and emotions can, at the same time, be great triggers to uncover negative meanings and ideas attached to words. That is why it is critical to become aware of what is going on inside of you. It is important to keep in mind that it is not always the outside circumstances that are creating your results in life. It is often your own negative thoughts, beliefs and feelings that prevent you from attracting what you really want in your life. What do you allow to interfere with your desire to create a great life?

What To Do Differently:

The first step is to increase your awareness. Your thinking has created the life you are living today, consciously or subconsciously. In order to create something different, start by analyzing your thoughts. What beliefs or thoughts are at the root of the results you created? Did negative thinking get in your way? Take a few minutes to ponder your answers. Even better, pull out your journal and write about each question. Journaling is very valuable—an in-depth process—that allows you to bring subconscious patterns to the surface by allowing your hand to simply write. You might be surprised at what comes up for you. Also, writing this information down supports consciously how you decide to change these undesired patterns.

There is also incredible power in journaling. When I was struggling to achieve my goals, journaling gave me insight into my thinking and beliefs around discipline. It helped me to see and change my own sabotaging behavior. I could feel the resistance, frustration, disappointment and the procrastination physically in my body until I discovered the true cause and made my subconscious work FOR me instead of against me. Learn to listen to your feelings so you can recognize your trigger points.

These are the action steps to support you in creating quantum shifts in your life, thereby allowing you to achieve your goals faster and with more ease:

Create a distraction-free environment for yourself:

This can be done almost anywhere. If you are good at tuning out noises, simply find a comfortable chair somewhere and tune out the world. If you need something more traditional, find a quiet and pleasant space, get comfortable in your favorite chair, let others know you are unavailable for a few minutes, and turn off the cell phone. You deserve a distraction-free environment. Give yourself permission to create this space for yourself in a way that is right for you.

Clear your mind and focus:

Take a few deep breaths, and as you breathe out, allow all the stress of the day to leave your body. Give yourself permission to set aside any pressing issues and decisions of the day, even if only for the next few minutes.

Create the question(s):

Take a few minutes to decide what your roadblock is. What are you resisting or procrastinating doing right now? What are you struggling with? What has been holding you back from achieving your goals? Become aware of the words that are affecting you negatively. In my case, I had an issue with discipline, so my question became, "Why am I struggling with discipline, in regards to obtaining my goals?"

Write in your journal:

After writing your question on the top of the page, allow your hand to write whatever comes up. When your hand chooses to stop writing, you are done. It is a very intuitive exercise. For example, when I did this exercise, my hand started writing about what my resistance to discipline really was. I realized that I had attached all kinds of negative meanings and thoughts to the word "discipline," like, "Discipline is hard work and no fun," "Discipline means giving up something good." When you have negative feelings about a word, it can create struggle and sabotage the actions you need to take to achieve your goals. Once you see clearly how your negative thoughts have been in your way, you will feel empowered to change your limiting thinking and behavior.

Redefining who you are:

The good news is attaching positive meanings to a word will support and empower you to achieve your goals. It is only a decision away. Recognizing that you can choose the meaning you attribute to any given word is a powerful realization.

For example, I changed the meanings and beliefs associated with the word "discipline" to:

☆ Discipline means joyfully following my daily and weekly plans to accomplish my goals.

☆ Being disciplined is exciting, exhilarating and empowering.

☆ Discipline means creating a healthy balance between work and play.

☆ I AM successful and great at being disciplined!

Now make a list of new meanings and thoughts describing your word by creating positive statements in the present tense.

Reinforcing the new You:

Next, make your positive statements visible so you can refer to them often. You can print them or write them on index cards. Be creative and make them eye catching. Post them next to your computer, on your fridge, even on the bathroom mirror, or carry your cards with you so you can read them several times a day. Read each one a minimum of five times every day for 30 days to reinforce and affirm the new "You"!

Repeat, as required:

Try these steps out on different words to see what you come up with. Have fun with this exercise. Use it as one of your tools to continually empower yourself, as you move forward in your life's journey.

Test Drive Your New Life:

When a situation happens that you do not like, do you get upset? Do you allow others to control your emotions? Even when there is nothing you can change about the situation, remain calm, in control of your emotions, and choose a positive approach. It does not have to ruin your mood and affect the rest of your day. There are usually several affirmative statements you can make about any event or situation. The same principal and steps can be used as in the "What To Do Differently" section. Simply re-phrase the question to reflect the event. In realizing this concept, you'll understand that you also have the same power to re-choose at any time.

Test it out for yourself. You will be amazed how good you will feel when you allow circumstances to just be circumstances.

Decide today to discover and release negative thoughts, beliefs and meanings holding you back. Make shifts to empower you in opening up avenues to the abundant life that you truly want to live. Search your heart, be as truthful as possible, and discover one thing today to release or shift, and move forward. Make a commitment to yourself to be ready, willing and open to new information, people and events that show up to move you in the directions that are right for you.

To support you in your quantum thinking for success, download your free workbook at www.results-that-matter.com/complimentaryworkbook, password is success. There is additional information in the workbook to support you through this process.

"I know that happiness, true authentic happiness, is an inside job that requires work and new information to reach and maintain new levels." Elizabeth J. Macarthur, Compassionate Samurai, Facilitator, Coach, Intuitive Guide

— ABOUT THE AUTHOR —

 Elizabeth J. Macarthur is a compassionate facilitator, coach and intuitive guide who assists individuals ready, open, and willing to remove key roadblocks. Inspire yourself to be an authority in your own life using self-directed, accountable growth techniques to achieve significant goals. See the true leader that you are. Be an extraordinary person today and make an extraordinary difference in your life and for humanity as a whole. For your free half-hour coaching session, contact Elizabeth today at elizabeth@results-that-matter.com or 587-989-6684. Move your life forward today at www.results-that-matter.com!

CHAPTER 28

Good Isn't Good Enough

Stephen Richardson

> *"You become what you think about."*
> – Earl Nightingale

Surprise! April Fool's day, 2004, would offer just that. I remember the day that changed my life forever, as if it was yesterday. It wasn't a practical joke I received, but another pink slip. For the third time in my 20+ year career as a retail store manager, I had been laid off. The conversation that I dreaded the most, the one telling my wife that our life had been turned upside down again, was but a painful commute away. It was that day I made a promise to myself and to my wife. I promised that I would NEVER get laid off again. That was a pretty bold statement during what would be the beginning of an historic economic recession. Bolder still was the realization that the only way to fulfill such a promise was never to work for someone else again.

Electrified with the prospect of a future free of "bosses," I decided to go one step further—I would live a more "significant" life. I had realized that over the course of my career, I had not been the husband or father I wanted to be. I had worked hard with little to show for it, because most of that hard work simply made someone else's dreams a reality. The exciting part was that I still had time to make a difference.

My goal for you is simple, yet very powerful! I challenge you, as I challenged myself on that fateful April day, to climb aboard the train to success, and by following a few simple steps, achieve YOUR excellence!

I had lived a good life, received a good education, had good jobs, and even a good home. All of that "good" in my life amounted to one thing: missed opportunities. The challenge with most "good" lives is that they rarely become great. I realized quickly that I shouldn't have been disappointed about being laid off from my good job, I should have been elated, because I had been given another chance to achieve greatness! I had spent countless hours studying successful people over the past two decades, but I had never implemented the four simple steps I was seeing over and over again in my own life.

The train to greatness has only five cars, but hold on tight, because this is the express route!

Step 1: Clearly define your goal

Not surprisingly, most people sabotage their own journey to success by not clearly defining their goals. You can go through life studying hard and working hard and, without a clear destination, fail. All of the great thought leaders throughout history have shared their version of this most critical first step. Earl Nightingale said, "We become what we think about," Napoleon Hill spoke of a "burning desire," and Stephen Covey famously taught us to "Begin with the end in mind." What did these men know that most of us don't? If you're not heading somewhere, you could end up anywhere. What are your goals for the next 30, 60, 90, and 120 days? If you don't know, STOP! Until you can answer this question, any bump on the track could stop you from achieving the greatness you were destined for.

Early in my consulting career, I decided the single most important thing I could do to further my business was to learn the art of communication. It was from that I decided my goal would be to become a master communicator through achieving the Distinguished Toastmaster Award from Toastmasters International.

Step 2: Have an obsessive desire

Obsession—the word evokes thoughts of a need so deep, nothing can stand between you and the thing you most desire. The concept is simple: If you don't want something badly enough, just about anything can prevent you from achieving it. Think about the things in your life you have achieved. Did you constantly talk, think, and dream about them? Did you eventually achieve those goals? Most people say, "Yes!"

Step 3: Develop a strong belief

No step in this process is more important—you must DEVELOP the belief that your goal will be achieved. You must believe that achieving your goal is only a matter of time! Belief is everything: without it, you will not fight through and weather the sacrifice and hardship that will undoubtedly come up along the way. A strong belief isn't something that just happens—you must DEVELOP it. Belief isn't a personality trait, it's just another skill mastered through practice. Learn and follow proven methods to develop and strengthen your ability to believe. Two of my favorite books on this are Claude M. Bristol's *The Magic of Believing* and David Joseph Schwartz's *The Magic of Thinking Big*.

Step 4: Identify a proven method

As kids, we were taught that we had to come up with the answers ourselves and had to figure most problems out alone. Fortunately, as adults we are allowed to learn from others and save a significant amount of time and effort. Find out what enabled others to achieve a goal like yours and take massive action to make it work.

To attain my goal, I not only followed the Toastmasters process, I turbo-charged it! What I accomplished in my first two years as a member of Toastmasters is something that most members do not accomplish in eight years. This massive action enabled me to reach Distinguished Toastmaster in record time. I don't write that to impress you. I write it to impress upon you what is possible when you follow this simple process. Short-term sacrifice toward a goal is infinitely easier than a long, drawn out effort, and the chances of reaching the goal increase as well.

Step 5: Be great!

Are you a Jack or Jill of All Trades? You aren't alone. Most people are good at a lot of things, but great at nothing. The reason for this is simple: people generally think it's good enough to be just good at everything. Be the best of the best at what you do and you will achieve great heights. Don't be a nameless face in the crowd. That is the crowd of people who don't get hired, who get passed over for promotions, or who get laid off at the first sign of economic uncertainty.

Pick a skill you can be great at and work hard to excel in it. According to experts on the topic, 10 years seems to be the magic time frame to master a skill. Whether that number is accurate or not, one thing is certain: mastering a skill requires a certain amount of time.

"Achieving Excellence is not only possible…
It's an Obligation!"

You have now come to the end of this chapter and might be thinking, "I've heard that before" or "That's nothing new or special" or "That's what everybody says about achieving goals."

Guess what? You're exactly right! Achieving goals is simple. Don't overthink it. Just do it!

My life has been totally transformed by applying the principles that I have just described. I am happier & more successful than ever. If I can do it, you can too!

Knowledge is basically worthless until it is applied. Therefore, I challenge you to re-read this chapter and make a commitment to complete the five steps listed, as they apply to your life. Invest the time to clearly define your goals. Never stop searching until you discover what you have an obsessive desire to achieve. Work hard to develop your skill of believing. Search for and then meticulously follow proven methods of success in your particular area of interest. And, finally, make a decision to be great at something.

— ABOUT THE AUTHOR —

 Stephen V. Richardson is a respected sales & communication expert as a result of his decades of service working with and for large & small companies spanning six countries and over 20 industries. He is a servant leader who loves to mentor & inspire others, especially youth. Stephen is also in high demand as a motivational speaker and business growth consultant. For more information or for a free business growth assessment, email ceo@stephenvrichardson.com or call 925-922-9000. facebook.com/stephenvrichardson

Limiting Beliefs

Limiting beliefs are
The constraints in your life,
Negative things said
That you anchor in your mind.

When you think you can do
Something wonderful and grand,
You pull a message from
Your thoughts to ruin your plan.

Make it a goal in your life
To overcome any doubt and fear,
Never second guess yourself
To allow limiting beliefs to interfere.

Fill your mind with positive thoughts
And your heart with the will to believe,
Your hopes, plans, goals and successes
Are meant for you to be achieved.

– Zenaida Roy-Almario

CHAPTER 29

Co-Create with the Universe and Expect Miracles

Margaret Child

> *"Whatever you can do or dream you can,*
> *begin it. Boldness has genius, power*
> *and magic in it. Begin it now."*
> – Goethe

*T*he lights are low and the energy in the room is palpable. I watch the antics of the people on stage with amazement and delight. I'm a little nervous. Soon it's going to be my turn! The foil-covered cardboard box I am wearing is not comfortable—I am anxious to be rid of it. I take a deep breath and burst onto the stage. I am a female version of R2D2 (of *Star Wars* fame), frantically calling out for my lover. Finally, frustration fries my circuits and I break out of the box to reveal the inner me in a Playboy Bunny outfit. With loud music playing, I let loose and dance wildly and freely until my audience are on their feet, clapping and cheering.

It's graduation night of a personal development class. After having been depressed for over four years, I have discovered that at the core of my being I am a beautiful spirit and a caring and powerful woman. I took this class when I was forty. I am now in my early seventies, but what I learned about the magnificence of the human spirit continues to inspire my life and work, to this day. (Not to mention the exhilarating experience of what it feels like to "break out of your box"!)

Have big dreams and set goals that expand the boundaries of "your box." When you realize the power that's available to you when you 'co-create with the Universe', you will be amazed at what you can achieve. The Universe wants every single one of us to be living our greatest joy and sharing our unique gifts, for the benefit of all.

Why Co-creating with the Universe is Important

When most people plan for the future, they are operating within the framework of PROBABILITY. Their ideas are based mainly on what has happened in the past to themselves or others. On the other hand, when you set goals, you make a statement to yourself and the Universe that you are willing to step outside of your comfort zone and play a bigger game. This takes you into the realm of POSSIBILITY. Yet, if you are ready to super-charge and magnify your goals. I'd like to invite you into the realm of UNLIMITED POSSIBILITIES. This is where the Universe acts most powerfully and you'll have the easiest access to the most expanded and creative ideas.

Let me share with you my favorite miracle story. After graduating from the Lifespring class mentioned above, I wanted to do my part in creating a better world. With a group of other people, I developed a weekly lunchtime lecture series, where local healers or spiritual teachers we had invited could talk about their work. The program was free and open to everyone—campus staff, students, and people in the neighborhood.

Inspired by what they shared, I decided that I wanted to do hands-on healing work fulltime and found myself drawn to Hellerwork, since it incorporates working with the wisdom of the body as well as the emotions. But I felt stuck. How could I possibly go from a well-paid job as a computer programmer to a completely new career, without ending up in the poor house? I couldn't see how I would ever achieve this goal. I fretted, planned and finally decided to hand it over to the Universe. I moved to a new department promising myself (and the Universe) that I would stay for two years and then be out of there.

Well, I didn't really keep my promise—three years later, I was still working in that same department. Until one day, out of the blue, my boss called me in his office. He informed me that I was going to be laid off. I was shocked and horrified. How could they do this to me? I left in a flood of tears and rushed home.

That evening, a longtime friend came over for dinner. I answered his knock on the door, obviously very upset. "What's the matter?" he asked. I blurted out the whole sad saga and he responded, excitedly, "Margaret, you have wanted to get out of that job for the longest time. Bring out the champagne! Let's celebrate!"

A miracle was staring me in the face and I didn't recognize it. In my wildest fantasies, I could not have come up with a sweeter deal than the one the Universe handed me. I got everything that I had asked for. The money from a generous severance package would pay for my one-year training in Hellerwork Structural Integration and even leave enough for me to live on! The training was fabulous and started me out on a journey of study and exploration of the human body and soul. It has been a joy and an honor to work with so many fabulous clients who taught me so much, and who benefitted from working with me, both physically and emotionally.

When you co-create with the Universe, be prepared for the wonderful and the unexpected, because *"Whatever you can do or dream you can, begin it. Boldness has genius, power and magic in it."*

How Co-creating Works

When you start to pursue a goal, know that you are automatically on a journey of self-discovery. There will be hurdles to overcome, but when you stay true to your course, you will develop and grow in ways that you can hardly imagine. You will notice how your self esteem will grow. Before you set your goals, though, ask yourself "What is it that I really want?" Often it's not "the thing" (i.e. the car, job, relationship, etc) that we want, but the feeling we expect to get from having it. What we really want is an on-going feeling of happiness and satisfaction.

Now is a very rich time to be alive. Take life on as a joyous adventure. Look for the opportunity in every challenge. We are all co-creating with the Universe anyway, but when we bring this into our conscious awareness, we'll experience the real magic and power.

> *"Whether you think you can, or you think you can't — you're right."*
> – Henry Ford

As I worked with my clients it became clear that people were looking for a map that would help them realize their dreams. That is why I have put together a program that helps people reach their goals in a unique way. In my 'Co-create with the Universe Program', we work through five key areas to help you:

1) Get crystal clear about what you want

Go beyond your imagined limitations to discover your biggest vision and deepest desires for your life and the world you want to live in.

2) Trust in yourself and the Universe

You are more powerful, more insightful, more brilliant than you realize. When you grow your self-esteem, develop your intuition and open up to the intelligence of the heart, you will be able to make better decisions.

3) Establish your goals and take action

Define your specific goals based on how you want to feel. Create space for inspiration. What steps are you willing to commit to?

4) Interact with the Universe

Contribute your best and pay attention to what the Universe is communicating to you.

5) Deal with doubts and fears

Your subconscious mind is enormously powerful. Befriend your subconscious mind so that it works for you instead of holding you back.

Let's take a look at overcoming doubts and fears for a moment. When I was 25, I discovered a neat trick. I grew up in England and I wanted to move to America, but I was afraid. My negative inner voice had kicked in: "This is just a silly fantasy. You don't have what it takes." In response, I put a message out to the Universe: "I need help."

Then I treated myself to the movie "Black Orpheus." The final scene left me feeling so energized and inspired that I announced, "I'm going to do it! I'm going to America!"

The negative voice was silenced in an instant. The Universe showed me how a high vibrational "YES!" state can drown out any negativity.

Does This Process Work for Relationships?

For all those who are looking for a loving relationship (and I looked for a long time), don't give up on your dreams. Become the best, most fulfilled person you can be so that you can bring a joyful and loving heart to whoever shows up. My husband and I have been together for over 27 years and are still having a lot of fun together. Even in our seventies we are still falling more and more in love, because I use the principles from my co-creating course.

In closing, I have a free gift for you. It's a fun exercise that you can use to raise your self esteem, to help you become a successful co-creator with the Universe. Go to: www.margaretchild.com/goals/self-esteem.html

— ABOUT THE AUTHOR —

Margaret Child has spent 20 years teaching individuals how to co-create with the Universe by teaching them how to trust their body's wisdom, honor their feelings, and expand their comfort zones. She is currently focused on getting her message out to a wider audience. She is an author and speaker, and leads workshops that help people find their unique gifts and shows them how to share them effectively in the world. Her signature program "Winning Over Worry" is available for groups and businesses to improve personal satisfaction and group productivity. www.margaretchild.com

CHAPTER **30**

Thoughts that Empower

Dennis Lund

> *"Throughout all history, the great wise men and teachers, philosophers, and prophets have disagreed with one another on many different things. It's only on this one point that they're in complete and unanimous agreement. We become what we think about."*
> – Earl Nightingale

Success is a personal choice. But think about it; how often do you take the time to define, connect with, and take action on your desires? You define what success is for you. The choices are unlimited, but you must be willing to overcome the challenges and pay the price. You will have many opportunities and many obstacles on your way, but you will succeed if you learn how to focus on a specific and clearly-defined goal and work your way to success. It is this process that allows you to grow, believe, and achieve.

When I refer to my personal success, I'm not talking about millions of dollars, but being in control of my own destiny. I enjoy a level of independence that I could not have experienced as an employee. It's important you learn to appreciate and enjoy the process, with its difficulties. It will build your confidence in the power of thought and in your abilities to create new successes.

Before you decide on your goals, it's crucial that you determine what success means to you. Like Stephen R. Covey says, "You don't want to climb a ladder to discover at the end that it's leaning towards the wrong building." At the age of 13, it was all about the money. Since then, I have come to realize that true success is much more, at least for me: it's more about fulfilling a sense of purpose and being of value to others. What is truly important in your life? What makes you happy? What brings you joy? Most people achieve success more easily when they follow their bliss, and wealth is often the result.

It can be that you have achieved a certain level of success. Maybe you have reached some of your goals and your life is pretty good. What if you could go to the next level? Where would you start? Begin by asking better and more powerful questions. Focus on new possibilities and new ways of being a person of value.

"Successful people ask better questions,
and as a result, they get better answers"
– Anthony Robbins

Why self-talk is so important — Thoughts are things

The private conversations you have with yourself have much more impact on your life and the world around you than you can ever imagine. The human brain is an incredible machine, but it is much more than that. Our subconscious mind acts as a conduit through which we may access infinite intelligence. Asking the right questions can provide us with the answers we need. Our subconscious mind will take a problem and wrestle with it until it comes up with a solution. It will then hand back that solution to our rational, thinking brain or conscious mind.

This may be what many refer to as an "Ah ha!" moment. Our brain is a tool that we use to reason, remedy, and remember with. It is also a tool that can purposefully shape and influence future events through deliberate and focused thoughts, affirmations, and the application of proper goal-setting techniques.

Like attracts like. As your brain is working and thinking, it is transmitting a signal or frequency that attracts similar thoughts. More and more like thoughts will come to you and when focused on for a long enough period of time, will begin to attract people, experiences, and circumstances that match your thoughts or frequency. When you set a goal or an intention, you are sending out a frequency. When you give your attention to something unwanted, you are sending out a frequency. Many people believe in a higher power, or an all-powerful, unseen force. How many times have you heard people say things like "God works in mysterious ways." "Be careful what you ask for." "The Universe responds differently to people with definite and deliberate plans." These are all references to the mysterious pulling power of thought. This mysterious, unseen force is sometimes referred to as "source" or "spirit."

"Spirit is a force and a mystery. All we know or may ever know of it is that it exists, and is ever working and producing all results in physical things seen of physical sense and many more not so seen. Thoughts are things."
– Prentice Mulford

Goals shape your self-talk

The importance of goal setting cannot be over emphasized. Goals move people to action! Without well-defined goals, chances are you'll get stuck in a rut. Creating goals and focusing on them will affect your self-talk and direct your subconscious mind to create new solutions. Most people focus on the How-To without first getting clear on what they want.

By setting goals, you help to bring your true desires into focus. Your thoughts and goals will set into motion a whole new world of possibilities for you, not only in your thinking but also in your reality. Goals are like the road map that keeps you on track, the glue that holds the puzzle pieces together when life bumps the table. They are not always perfect but you will eventually get to your destination. Remember that you have a choice. Be confident in your ability to work out any problem. There is no such thing as failure as long as you are willing to accept responsibility for your circumstances and direct your thoughts and actions.

> *"Our doubts are traitors and make us lose the good we oft might win by fearing to attempt."*
> — William Shakespeare

Create a vision that excites you. When your goals support your vision or purpose, they become more fulfilling and sustainable. They will give you clarity on the actions to take. If you need some help getting started, read a biography of someone past or present that inspires you, or find a coach or mentor. Goal setting really is the best tool to create change as we become what we think about. Keep looking in the direction that you want to go. Have fun with it!

The game is so much more fun when you understand it: it is no longer about struggling and being a victim of your circumstances; it is about experiencing and enjoying your own creative processes. Your experiences will elevate you to new levels of awareness. You'll discover that with every corner you turn, you will be gifted with new information and new ideas that will help you in the process. Whenever you feel stuck, review your vision and your goals to ensure that you are on track. You may attract books, opportunities and people who can introduce you to new ideas and strategies.

With a clear vision, you will continue to focus your attention and thoughts on what you want, you'll set powerful goals and get into action! Enjoy each and every step of your path!

I am extremely grateful for the difference my coach has made in my life and I'd like to pay it forward and offer you, the reader of this book, a free 30-minute coaching session. (Please email me at info@askdennislund.com.)

— ABOUT THE AUTHOR —

Dennis Lund is an extraordinary entrepreneur and businessman with more than 20 years experience. As a Certified Professional Performance Coach, Dennis uses his broad knowledge and expertise to assist business professionals, entrepreneurs, and individuals in their quest to live their vision. Dennis Lund enjoys being a speaker and a coach, because he believes this is his greatest opportunity to be of service to others and to create change in the world. www.askdennislund.com

CHAPTER 31

Don't Quit Until Your Vision is Reality

Patrick Ciriello

> *Vision without action is a daydream.*
> *Action without vision is a nightmare.*
> – Japanese Proverb

"Set up the board, but leave your queen in the box," said my grandfather one Saturday afternoon, in the fall of 1972. Over the summer, my grandfather had been teaching me the basics of playing chess. "But I can't play without my queen," I answered. "It's the most important piece."

"No," said my grandfather, with a slight smile and a look that was slightly mischievous, "the most important piece is the king. If you lose the king, you lose the game. So you must learn how to defend your king."

And so we played. I had no queen, and in the first few games I got slaughtered. But every time, with every move, my grandfather showed me why it had been a mistake and what I should have done instead. After several months, I began to develop tactics and strategies that didn't require the queen. In fact, when I was finally allowed to use the queen again, I barely used her except when necessary and it was usually to take out one of my opponent's major pieces, as a sacrifice. I had learned to think a lot more creatively. I was able to see the board from many other perspectives, just as a general must do on the field of battle. And I learned the principals of sacrifice and patience. Not easy things to teach an eight-year-old! I became the best chess player in school. My fondness of the game diminished significantly a few years later when my grandfather passed away. But the lessons he taught me have stayed with me my whole life.

Remember when I said "I can't?" My grandfather didn't say anything; he just assumed that I could. I used that phrase again, a few years later—it was the last time I ever did. I was taking one of my first trumpet lessons and I was frustrated with a particular passage of music. I put my trumpet down and said, "I can't do it." Never will I forget the expression on my music teacher's face. She gently grabbed my arm, looked me straight in the eye, and said, "I never want to hear that word again. Take it out of your vocabulary." I was stunned, but it stuck with me. I played the passage, and eventually became one of the best musicians in school. To this day, I have never again used the word "can't," nor shall I ever. Our early experiences contribute significantly to the direction of our lives—in my case, I was taught never to quit, and I don't.

To be successful, you need four things: Vision, a plan, a can-do attitude, and you must involve others. Life is all about learning and change. Failure only comes when you quit learning, or you quit dreaming. So don't quit. Find your vision—borrow someone else's, if you must—and make that vision a reality. Along the way, the vision may change or may be replaced by another one. That's ok. As you learn more and involve more people in your life and in your goals, this is inevitable. In the following pages, I want to share with you some of the lessons I have learned. Some were easy, and came from unexpected sources. Some I learned the hard way. I hope my own journey will inspire you as you pursue your own.

When you hit the inevitable brick walls, you need something that can sustain you when you feel like quitting. A can-do, never-quit attitude will help. Thinking creatively will help. But you also need to have the fuel and foundation necessary to keep going, long before the challenges come. You need to have a vision.

Your vision is something beyond your imagination—something so profound, so expansive, so wonderful, it's almost scary to contemplate. That vision encompasses all aspects of your life: career, family, friends, hobbies, where you live, how you live, and with whom you spend your time. Once you have that clear vision, you can work backwards, tracing the steps in reverse order back to where you first started. Reversing the process becomes your pathway—you can start planning what you need to do to move forward in all aspects of your life. Those become your short-term, medium-term, and long-term goals. You create a plan: what will I do today, what will I do tomorrow, what will I do next week, next month, and next year to achieve my goals?

To find your vision and make it your reality, you need to remember:
☆ Never to say "I can't."
☆ Nothing is impossible.
☆ Challenges must be faced strategically, tactically, and creatively.
☆ Everything is about relationships.

It has taken me a very long time to realize that at the end of the day, everything is about relationships—whether in your personal or professional life—and it is your strongest relationships that will help you move forward when times get difficult. Adding this to the mix of the vision, creative thinking, and the belief that nothing is impossible will help to set the next stage of your own journey. No one succeeds on their own: it always involves a team. Fortunately, putting such a team together is not that difficult. Most people are willing to jump in and help someone else; it is part of human nature. Share your goals with others, and you will find those who want the same things.

You see, your vision is really a projection of yourself. You need to see the "best" image of yourself in order to really develop your vision. For me, it is a combination of past versions of "me," where I have been successful, and an overlay of the present "me" on images that portray my vision of the future. There has always been one image I've had in mind of myself, ever since I was a small boy. The vision is of me, sitting in the command chair of the Starship Enterprise. You see, my vision all along has been a world where peace reigns, fear doesn't exist, poverty and hunger and disease have been eradicated, and the people of the world simply live to be the best version of themselves possible. What is your vision? What is it that has been in the back of your mind since you were a child? What impact do you want to have on the world, or even in just your own neighborhood?

I have been on quite a journey over the past 40 years. For too long, however, I was overly focused on myself. Now, I take that experience and guide others through their own journey. There are many people who are creative and imaginative but have never developed a vision. When you don't have a vision, you have no destination, and so all you will be doing is spinning your wheels, going around in circles. Without goals, it's easy to resort to the way you have always done things, especially when facing new challenges.

Just as any professional athlete or athletic team needs a coach or guide, so do individuals, entrepreneurs, business owners, and just regular people. My vision is to help you develop your own vision, develop your own plans and goals for success, learn to see the world from many perspectives, and build the relationships necessary for you to become "your best self." In a matter of weeks, my life changed dramatically. Yours can, too.

Send an email to visionbook@hawksmountain.com to claim your free gift. The best part of your life is still ahead of you. Let me help you find your vision, set your goals, and make your mark in this world. Call 888.236.8015 to schedule your complimentary coaching session.

Find Your Vision - Make It Reality.™

— ABOUT THE AUTHOR —

 Patrick Ciriello is a coach, speaker, author, and business consultant. A serial entrepreneur for over 20 years, Patrick has helped large corporations develop systems that, to this day, are keeping food on the shelves for millions of people and the price of medications for millions of others affordable. He now helps others to develop their vision, define their goals, map out their plans, and guides them along the pathway to success. Whether you want to enhance your career, start a business, or simply live a better life, a vision of your future is the place to start. www.hawksmountain.com

CHAPTER 32

From Hope to Prosperity

Wayne Kotomori

> *"For I know the plans I have for you, is the utterance of Jehovah, "plans to prosper you and not to harm you, plans to give you hope and a future."*
> — Jeremiah 29:11

*I*magine that you are in a canoe race. You are eager to win—in fact, you have been training for months, perhaps even years, for this moment. Although you are rowing as hard as you can, you look around at the other boats dotting the surface of the water and realize that you are falling behind. Not only are they beginning to outpace you, but despite all of your intensive training, you are starting to run out of energy. You begin to despair that you will ever even finish the race, let alone place well. Your hope is fading. In this economy, you could feel similarly about your hopes of succeeding in business or finding employment. But it doesn't have to be that way.

About a year ago, I was laid off from my job with the Federal Government—and through this experience, I found freedom. My job had been to help others find jobs. When people get laid off, it affects them because they lose a sense of their value, their identity. They would come in with their heads down, heartbroken; a lot of them were one month away from living on the street. The only jobs available were minimum wage jobs in various service fields, which are rarely ever an adequate means of support. They needed more than that. They needed a career. There were hardly any promising jobs available, though, and when one did appear, there would be hundreds of applicants vying for it. I couldn't always help them find a job. But I gave them something even more valuable—I helped them realize that there was still hope.

No matter what situation you find yourself in, you can get through it if you have hope. Even 0.00000001% of hope is better than none. Nobody can live without it. Even if it's just that 0.00000001%, you can succeed. Realize that no matter how dark the reality of your life today may be, as long as you keep hope within you, all is not lost.

That is a lesson we can learn from the illustration of the canoe race: as long as you don't give up and keep rowing, you can finish the race— or maybe even win. You wouldn't get in a canoe and start rowing in the first place if you didn't have at least a little hope of winning. Nobody is going to do it for you; it's something that you have to go out and make happen on your own.

The best way to take control of your life is to build your own business, to be your own boss. That's how you can make your dreams come true. One way you can do this is through network marketing, where the systems are already in place. Regardless of what you want to achieve in life, you always need a team. How do you build a successful team?

Let's look at three different types of "business canoe teams."

1   **The One-Man Canoe**—In this case, all you have are your own ideas, your own goals, and only the manpower that you yourself can provide, as you paddle towards the finish line. Unfortunately for some people, their egos can get the better of them, here: they want to stand on their own merit and do things their own way. They don't want to listen to others or rely on anybody but themselves. People who do this, though, are missing out on valuable input, as well as limiting their possibilities and their goals. Without other people helping them, other resources to draw on, their business stands a greater chance of failing.

2 **The Two-Man Canoe**—In the two-man canoe, two people are working together to reach the finish line. But what if there is not one unified vision? What if both people have their own ideas of how to reach the finish line or even in which direction to go? Rather than helping each other, they could be allowing their egos to get in the way—they could be competing with each other. Business partners exist to lift each other up, not to knock each other down, instead of paddling in opposite directions. You would be wasting valuable energy and getting nowhere.

3 **The 13-Man Canoe**—On this team, each member brings something different to the table, and they each contribute it towards the good of the team. They are willing to work together, to team up and share resources. Every member buys into the concept. In a company, the business owner is the one who has to pull everyone together, draw on their talents, give them directions, and show them how to operate as a team. In the bigger picture, you want God to be the leader who guides and directs your team. When there is direction, businesses will prosper. This is a team of 13 people who undergo intensive training together for years, until they are all in sync with each other, in every aspect. And I'm not just referring to the twelve who are paddling, but also to the one in the back who is shouting out the directions. They will win the race, for sure.

So how can you build your own canoe team? The answer is to surround yourself with like-minded people, and make sure you all share a common purpose or need. Somebody can have the greatest vision, the greatest goals, and someone in their personal life can keep them from reaching it. You can have the brightest people on your team, but if they can't work together, it's useless. They need to understand that everybody can win. You have to be able to lead the team, to make them buy into this philosophy.

You need people with talent. Nobody is good at everything. You need people on your team who can do the things that you can't. Maybe that means enlisting someone who can provide financing or expertise in marketing, or with a background in HR. Perhaps they only have these individual skills, but when you put them together. . . hey, what a great team! Then, they can come in and train other people, when the company grows.

But what if you don't feel confident in your ability to lead? How do you develop leadership skills?

☆ Change your thought process. Remember the proverb, "As a man thinketh in his heart, so is he." What you envision is very possible, when you believe in yourself. You have to believe in yourself before anybody else can.

☆ Go to leadership seminars to discover your potential and become a better leader.

☆ Learn from your past experiences. What mistakes have you made that you can learn from?

☆ With great power comes great responsibility. The leader has to determine the direction of the company. It's important to delegate responsibilities.

☆ Surround yourself with strong leaders and positive thinking people who have goodness in their hearts.

☆ Reach out to help other people. Ask them "How can I support you in your business? How can we work together? How can I build you up?" When people notice you care, they will reciprocate. Don't think about what you will gain; ask how you can enrich other people and their businesses. Focus on what you can give rather than what you would like to get.

Even though I failed in two businesses and the general thought was, "You'll never succeed," I never gave up hope. Between my overprotective mother and two failed marriages, I was afraid for a long time of trying anything new, because I didn't want to fail.

A few months ago, my second wife and I decided to file for divorce. It wasn't an easy decision to make, but since I've left her, my hopes for the future are skyrocketing. A new world has opened up for me. I can see my own vision; I can go my own way. I'm building my 13-man canoe team, surrounding myself with people of good character, and forming my own master plan. I'm transforming my hope into prosperity—and so can you!

— ABOUT THE AUTHOR —

Wayne Kotomori is a transition coach, assisting in connecting you to your dream, plan, prosperity, hope, future. Giving people hope is a vital part of what he offers. His goal is to create jobs by helping people start and grow their business. He has launched the Jeremiah Foundation to create a National Coalition of Veterans. When you feel inspired by his chapter and want to join his 13-man canoe team, visit www.Jeremiahfoundation.net or email Wayne JeremiahFnd@gmail.com.